THE
BOOK
OF
CHRISTMAS

THE

BOOK

OF

CHRISTMAS

EVERYTHING WE ONCE KNEW AND
LOVED ABOUT CHRISTMASTIME

JANE STRUTHER

THE
BOOK
OF
CHRISTMAS

EVERYTHING WE ONCE KNEW AND
LOVED ABOUT CHRISTMASTIME

JANE STRUTHERS

EBURY
PRESS

5 7 9 10 8 6 4

First published in 2012 by Ebury Press, an imprint of Ebury Publishing
A Random House Group company

The Random House Group Limited Reg. No. 954009

Addresses for companies within the Random House Group can be found at
www.randomhouse.co.uk

A CIP catalogue record for this book is available from the British Library

The Random House Group Limited supports the Forest Stewardship Council®
(FSC®), the leading international forest-certification organisation. Our books
carrying the FSC label are printed on FSC®-certified paper. FSC is the only
forest-certification scheme supported by the leading environmental
organisations, including Greenpeace. Our paper procurement policy can be
found at www.randomhouse.co.uk/environment

Printed and bound by CPI Group (UK) Ltd, Croydon, CR0 4YY

ISBN 9780091947293

To buy books by your favourite authors and register for offers visit
www.randomhouse.co.uk

In fond memory of my grandparents,
Maud and Leonard Struthers,
who did so much to put the magic
into my childhood Christmases

CONTENTS

CONTENTS

FOREWORD

Heap on more wood! – the wind is chill;
But let it whistle as it will,
We'll keep our Christmas merry still.

'MARMION', SIR WALTER SCOTT

Everyone has their own idea of the perfect merry Christmas. It might be snowy or sunny, steeped in religious meaning or completely secular, an opportunity for total relaxation or some frenetic socialising, a time when old enmities are forgotten or new ones are created. No matter how we choose to spend our Christmas, it gives us another memory that we can look back on in years to come, just as our parents had, and their parents before them, and all the other countless generations going right back to the time when Christmas was first celebrated. And some of our collective memories go back even further than this.

In our artificially illuminated, non-stop world, it is easy to become cut off from the natural course of each season. In mid-December, especially for those of us living in southern Britain, we may not notice that the hours of daylight have shrunk so much that they have reached the darkest point of the winter solstice. Our ancestors, reliant on candles, lanterns and fires, felt gratitude and relief at the knowledge that the days would begin to lengthen again and the sun's strength would return. Their lives depended on it, and they celebrated the start of another year with feasting and games long before the birth of Christ. Some of these age-old midwinter festivals still influence the way we celebrate the Twelve Days of Christmas, even if we aren't aware of the fact.

The Book of Christmas explores many of these old traditions and activities, from the Roman Saturnalia to medieval mumming, from the antics of the Lord of Misrule to the strictures of the Puritans, from royal excesses to the trials of keeping Christmas when there's a war on. The book tells of angelic visitations, wise men from the east, the star and the stable. There are crackers and trees, candles and gifts, carols and entertainments, feasts and treats, joys and tribulations. And, just like finding those final presents hidden in the toe of a Christmas stocking, there is a lot more besides – ancient superstitions, cherished customs, favourite Christmas stories, not to mention folklore, ghosts, sprites and strange legends. A blend of the comforting and the curious.

All the ingredients, in fact, for a delightfully merry Christmas and a happy New Year.

Jane Struthers
East Sussex

ECHOES FROM THE PAST

The fairest season of the passing year –
The merry, merry Christmas time is here.

'THE MERRY CHRISTMAS TIME', GEORGE ARNOLD

MIDWINTER REVELS

L ate December, when the hours of daylight are short and much of nature appears to have gone to sleep, is one of the most important turning points of the year in the northern hemisphere. It is the time of the winter solstice, when the sun appears to be stationary in the sky (and, in the higher latitudes, almost completely disappears) before the days gradually begin to lengthen and the natural world wakes up once more. It's the perfect opportunity to cheer ourselves up with a monumental party and, for those of us with a sense of the spiritual in the middle of the mundane, to honour something greater than ourselves. This celebration has been enjoyed for millennia, in one guise or another.

☙ Saturnalia ❧

Anyone who complains about the riotous nature of office Christmas parties, or who looks askance at the bottles of alcohol in other people's supermarket trolleys, might like to reflect that there is nothing new about having a wild time during the winter solstice. The ancient Romans were particularly good at it, as they were with so many other things, and really threw themselves into their own midwinter celebrations, which they called Saturnalia. When they invaded Britain (the first successful invasion was in 54 BC), they brought their practices with them, and these included Saturnalia.

The festival of Saturnalia was dedicated to the Roman god Saturn, who ruled over agriculture. At the darkest time of the year, when many crops and plants had disappeared underground or died off completely, the Romans wanted to honour their god so he would be pleased with them and bring them good harvests in the coming year. They also had a sense of nostalgia, and Saturnalia was an echo of how they thought life was lived in the time of Saturn.

The festival began each year on 17 December, which was a day devoted to religious rites. Everyone went to the temple, where the woollen bands that normally secured the feet of the statue of Saturn were loosened so he could join in the celebrations, and the priests performed sacrifices. After this, there was a public banquet. Everything – from schools to businesses and law courts – closed down during Saturnalia, and no work was done. Instead, the Romans occupied themselves with the serious business of drinking, eating, dancing, celebrating and cavorting in as uninhibited a fashion as humanly possible. Each social group also elected a man who was the master of ceremonies during Saturnalia, issuing dares and overseeing all the jollity. He was possibly a forerunner of the medieval Lord of Misrule, who was elected to preside over the celebrations at Christmas.

Something else that marked out Saturnalia from the rest of the year was that the social order was turned on its head. Slaves, who were usually respectful and obeyed orders, became the masters. All sorts of activities that were normally forbidden, such as drinking and gambling, were open to them. The masters, whose word was usually law, took the subservient role, serving food to their slaves and carrying out their wishes.

The Romans also exchanged gifts during Saturnalia but often specifically on 23 December, which was known as Sigillaria. Their gifts were more usually tokens of friendship, such as wax or pottery figures, and candles, rather than lavish displays of wealth which would have run contrary to the topsy-turvy nature of the season.

Everyone had so much fun that it's no wonder Saturnalia was gradually extended from a single day to a three-day festival, and finally to one that ran until 23 December. Unofficially, it often lasted longer than that, rather in the way that the Christmas holidays are frequently extended today.

∼ The unconquered sun ∼

The Romans of the third century celebrated 25 December as *Dies natalis Solis Invicti* – the birthday of the unconquered sun. In 274, the Roman emperor Aurelian declared it to be a major holy day in honour of Sol, the sun god. Opinion is divided on whether this was the start of a new Roman cult or whether it was a revival of an older Syrian cult. Either way, it didn't last long and the figure of Sol disappeared from the face of Roman coinage in 324, during the reign of Constantine, the first Christian Roman emperor.

Before long, both Saturnalia and *Dies natalis Solis Invicti* belonged to the past, and Romans once again had something new to celebrate each 25 December – the birth of the son of God, rather than the birthday of the unconquered sun.

∼ Yule ∼

Did Britons once celebrate a midwinter festival called Yule before Christianity became established? No one is quite sure. Some authorities claim it was a pre-Christian midwinter festival that originated in Scandinavia and came over to Britain with the Vikings.

Others believe it is simply an early name for Christmas. (The first recorded use of the word 'Christmas' occurred in the twelfth century.) The etymology of 'Yule' is complicated and obscure, but we do know that in Old English it was *geol* (plus many variations), and it may be linked with the Danish *juul*, thereby having some connection with the Danish rule of England in the eleventh century.

The name 'Yule' stuck in northern England and Scotland, where it is still more likely to be used than in the rest of Britain. Yule is also remembered in the Yule log – once the special log that was chosen to burn on Christmas Day, and now more commonly the chocolate roulade that is often eaten as an alternative to Christmas pudding.

Sometimes, extracting the truths about ancient festivals from the popular myths surrounding them is rather like trying to separate the individual ingredients in an overcooked Christmas pudding. They get stuck together, making it difficult to analyse them, and some have lost their original identity altogether and become something else. That seems to be true of Yule.

MAKING A DATE

We've always celebrated Christmas on 25 December, haven't we? Well, no, we haven't. During the very early days of Christianity, no date was set for the birth of Christ and the Bible certainly didn't give any clues. In fact, many bishops and other Church elders disagreed wholeheartedly with the notion of celebrating the birthdays of Christian martyrs. That was pagan nonsense! The day to be celebrated was the anniversary of the saint's martyrdom. This is why the date for Easter (even though it's a moveable feast) was settled long before the date for Christmas.

Over the following centuries, various possible dates for Christ's birth were discussed by religious scholars, with many believing that it took place in the spring: 21 March, 15 April, 20 or 21 April and 20 May were all contenders. The conundrum slowly started to resolve itself, and by the fourth century only two possible dates were considered for Christ's birth, even though neither had been mooted in the previous discussions. Christians in the western Roman Empire celebrated Christ's birth on 25 December, while Christians in the eastern Roman Empire preferred 6 January. This period spans what are now known as the Twelve Days of Christmas, beginning with what is considered to be Christmas Day in most areas of the Christian world and ending with Epiphany on 6 January.

The burning question is why Christian scholars eventually settled on 25 December in the first place. There are two possible reasons. The first is that the Christian Church wanted to make a connection between the new feast day and the Roman feast of *Dies natalis Solis Invicti* ('the birthday of the unconquered sun'). Presumably, it was thought that people would be more receptive to Christianity if they were still allowed to have a riotous time at the darkest point of the year.

The other possibility is connected to the Jewish festival of Passover. It was once believed that Jesus died on the anniversary of his conception, in common with all the other saints. The date set for Passover was 25 March and therefore, reasoned the theologists as they counted nine months ahead, Jesus was born on 25 December.

Ultimately, of course, we don't know for certain why Christmas now falls on 25 December. Neither do we know which day of the year was Jesus's real birthday. It will probably remain a mystery for ever.

THE CHRISTMAS CALENDAR

Anyone who complains today that the Christmas holiday is too long might be surprised to know that it has always been a protracted affair. Our ancestors began thinking and planning for the festival weeks in advance, and made various preparations for it on set days, all of which were given special names.

The dates of the Twelve Days of Christmas were fixed during the Council of Tours (a meeting of officials of the Roman Catholic Church, held in Tours in France) in 567. Although the twelve-day period was one of merriment, only three days were designated as official feast days: Christmas Day, New Year's Day and Epiphany.

❧ All Hallows Eve – 31 October ❧

This was when the Lord of Misrule was chosen for the forthcoming Christmas festivities.

❧ Martinmas Day – 11 November ❧

A day of feasting and jollity, which coincided with the annual slaughtering of livestock in preparation for the winter months of hardship. Between the sixth and ninth centuries this feast day preceded the strict forty-day Advent fast that began the following day. The feast day of Martinmas continued after the ninth century, but the forty-day fast did not and was dropped in favour of the shorter Advent season that we have today.

❧ Stir-up Sunday – Last Sunday before Advent ❧

The Sunday in late November on which every self-respecting cook and housewife once prepared their Christmas puddings. Its name comes from the first words of that Sunday's Collect in the Book of Common Prayer.

❧ Advent Sunday ❧

This is the first Sunday in the Advent season that we observe today. Depending on the date on which Easter falls, Advent Sunday can be as early as 27 November and as late as 3 December.

❧ St Nicholas's Day – 6 December ❧

Not only is this the traditional day for children to post their requests to Father Christmas (preferably by putting them up the chimney), in medieval times it was the day when English choirboys elected one of their fellow choristers as a boy bishop.

❧ St Thomas's Day – 21 December ❧

This was once the day when the adult members of each parish would give small amounts of money to their poorer elderly neighbours. This was known as 'Thomasing' or 'mumping'. If the money wasn't forthcoming, the elderly people were allowed to ask for it. The same rule applied to children, who were entitled to ask for corn or apples.

❧ Christmas Eve – 24 December ❧

In previous centuries, this was the final day of the Christmas fast –
and it still is for those who regard Advent as a period of abstinence.
It was also the day when people decorated their houses in readiness
for Christmas by bringing in evergreens and the Yule log.

❧ Christmas Day – 25 December ❧

This is the first of the Twelve Days of Christmas. It has long been a
feast day, and was once the day when people were allowed to eat
meat and fish again after their long and severe Advent fast.

❧ St Stephen's Day – 26 December ❧

St Stephen was the first Christian martyr to die following Christ's
crucifixion. His day is now more commonly known in the United
Kingdom as Boxing Day.

❧ Holy Innocents' Day – 28 December ❧

Also known as Childermas, this commemorates Herod's slaughter of
all children in Bethlehem aged two or under, in his attempt to kill the
young Jesus. It was once considered a solemn and unlucky day within
the general Christmas jollities. It was also the day on which the boy
bishops, who had been appointed on St Nicholas's Day, reigned
supreme in some religious institutions.

❧ New Year's Eve – 31 December ❧

Known as Hogmanay in Scotland, this celebration sees out the old
year and greets the new one. The passing of the old year is often
marked by the tolling of church bells and also by many traditions,
including opening all the windows of the house at the stroke of
midnight to let out the old year.

New Year's Day – 1 January

Traditionally, this was the second feast day
during the Christmas period. Until the early
seventeenth century, it was also the day on
which people exchanged gifts.

Epiphany – 6 January

This was the third and final Christmas feast day. It commemorates the
arrival of the Magi, or Three Wise Men, at the stable where the infant Jesus
lay. The sacred festival of Epiphany was gradually overshadowed by the
more secular celebration of Twelfth Night, which once involved much
revelry and feasting to mark the end of the Christmas season. Twelfth Night
was originally celebrated on 5 January but the date has slipped and Twelfth
Night now takes place on what was once Twelfth Day.

Plough Monday – First Monday
after Epiphany

As far as agricultural workers were concerned, this was the beginning
of the new working year. From the fifteenth century onwards, candles
were burnt in churches on this day to ask for God's blessing on all who
worked on the land. Not that they did much work on Plough Monday,
because they were much too busy with a variety of enjoyable and traditional celebrations. The hard work resumed the following day.

St Distaff's Day – First Tuesday
after Epiphany

The men had their fun on Plough Monday, and it was the women's
turn the next day, which is St Distaff's Day. This was traditionally the
day when women took up their spinning duties after the Christmas
celebrations although, as with Plough Monday, they were having so
much fun that their spinning took a very poor second place.

❧ Candlemas – 2 February ❧

Until Victorian times, this was the day on which everyone took down their Christmas decorations. Candlemas commemorates the Purification of the Virgin Mary after Christ's birth.

THE LORD OF MISRULE

I n medieval and Tudor times, the Christmas activities at court, universities and in the great houses of the nobility were organised by the Lord of Misrule. He was elected specially for the purpose and he had a host of helpers. The general idea was for the Lord of Misrule to create as much merriment as possible, and often to whip up some enjoyable festive chaos at the same time. It was yet another example of the tradition, which stemmed from the Roman Saturnalia, of reversing the natural order of things at Christmas.

The Tudor kings were particular fans of the Lord of Misrule. From 1489 until the end of his reign, Henry VII's Christmases were overseen by not only a Lord of Misrule but also an Abbot of Unreason. When he succeeded to the throne in 1509, Henry VIII kept up the tradition of having a Lord of Misrule. His son, Edward VI, appointed the last royal Lord of Misrule, who was George

Ferrers. Ferrers had his own lavish retinue, which included an astronomer, and one Christmas he 'materialised' out of a moon.

The custom of appointing a royal Lord of Misrule fizzled out when Edward VI died in 1553. Mary, his half-sister and successor, abandoned the practice but kept a Master of Revels to preside over her own Christmases. The demise of the Lord of Misrule at court encouraged the fashionable aristocracy to abandon the practice as well, although some well-heeled members of the gentry still enjoyed it. It also continued to flourish in the Inns of Court in London, leading to some very rowdy scenes. However, even these were quenched by the deluge of cold water that the Puritans poured over Christmas in the 1640s. Although Christmas was reinstated in 1660, no one had any interest in reviving a tradition that turned everything on its head. Perhaps they had experienced too much of inverted reality for that.

FROM JULIAN TO GREGORY

There are some strange anomalies concerning Christmas, such as why Twelfth Night was once celebrated on 5 January by some people and on 6 January by others. And what do people mean when they talk about Old Christmas Day?

❧ The Julian calendar ❧

All these mysteries are solved when we consider what happened in Britain in September 1752. Until then, the year was organised according to the Julian calendar, which was so-named after Julius Caesar who had instigated it in 45 BC. It was a solar calendar, consisting of 365¼ days divided into twelve months of roughly thirty days each, and with an extra day every four years. This was a vast improvement on the previous Roman system of a lunar-based calendar, with each year lasting for 355 days, but it still wasn't perfect.

☙ The Gregorian calendar ☙

Despite its flaws, the Julian calendar worked well enough to be getting on with. However, what had originally been tiny inaccuracies by a few minutes each year gradually accumulated over the centuries into a major slippage of time. In 1582, Pope Gregory XIII, who led the Roman Catholic world, announced a way to rectify all these problems. His plan included cutting ten days out of October that year, with the result that the date jumped from 4 October to 15 October. Why October? Because it has few holy days, so there was no danger of omitting any.

The Roman Catholic countries obediently switched to the new Gregorian calendar, as it was called, on the appointed date or soon afterwards, but Protestant countries refused to abide by what they considered to be a Popish plot. This meant that Europe was divided by two completely different calendars, which caused much confusion. For over a century, Britain held out against the apparently crazy edict of the man deemed the 'Roman Antichrist' before it finally had to bow to the inevitable. This came in 1752, by which time it was necessary to lose eleven days rather than the ten that had been proposed two centuries before, because the Gregorian calendar had ignored the leap year of 1700 while the Julian calendar had observed it. So, in Britain and her colonies, the early days of September 1752 duly ran from 2 September to 14 September. What is more, the official start of each year changed from 25 March to 1 January, in line with the new Gregorian calendar.

☙ Old versus New Style ☙

Dates from the Julian calendar were referred to as 'Old Style', while dates from the Gregorian calendar were known as 'New Style'. In Britain, we still have an annual reminder of this switch from the

Julian calendar. The beginning of the British tax year falls on 6 April (which seems such an arbitrary date), because that is the Old Style official start of the year when translated into the New Style of the Gregorian calendar.

❧ Christmas and the new calendar ❧

Despite its accuracy, the switch to the Gregorian calendar still produced a muddle in Britain because some people embraced the new system while others clung stubbornly to the old one. This led to many disgruntled mutterings.

Traditionalists were particularly wary about changing the day on which they celebrated festivals. This meant that Christmas Day was still celebrated on 25 December, but some people observed it on what would have been the Julian date (6 January in the new calendar, which they called 'Old Christmas Day' because it was 25 December in the old calendar) while others preferred to forget the past and follow the new Gregorian date.

Even the Glastonbury thorn, which is associated with Joseph of Arimathea and traditionally flowers on Christmas Eve, was brought into the argument. Much to the satisfaction of a man called John Latimer living in Bristol, the thorn 'contemptuously ignored the new style' by flowering on 5 January, 'thus indicating that Old Christmas Day should alone be observed, in spite of an irreligious legislature'. Yet, elsewhere in the country, cuttings of the original thorn were apparently flowering merrily on the new Christmas Day. It seems that the thorn was as confused as everyone else.

❧ The Twelve Days of Christmas ❧

The fact that the number of missing days was similar to the Twelve Days of Christmas only added to the chaos over the Old and New Style Christmas feasts. In time, Old Christmas Day (Old Style 6 January) became caught up with Twelfth Day (New Style 6 January), which gradually changed its name to Twelfth Night (originally celebrated on New Style 5 January). No wonder so many people regarded Twelfth Night as an opportunity to make as merry as possible – they could blame the mix-up on strong drink and too much dancing.

THE WINTER SOLSTICE

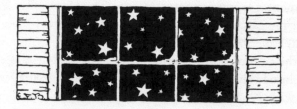

We have been enjoying celebrations of the winter solstice, in one form or another, for millennia. It is clearly a very good time of year for a party. But the winter solstice also has important astronomical significance and is one of the turning points during the solar calendar.

≈ The sun stands still ≈

The word 'solstice' comes from the French, which in turn is derived from the Latin *solstitium*. *Sol* means 'the sun', and *stistere* means 'to stop' or 'to stand'. So its literal meaning is that the sun stands still.

In order to understand the winter solstice, we first have to comprehend the relationship between the sun and the earth.

≈ The annual path of the sun ≈

From our perspective on earth, the sun appears to travel around our planet. The reality, of course, is that the sun is at the centre of our solar system and all the planets, including the earth, rotate around it – a discovery that landed Galileo, among other astronomers, in an awful lot of trouble with the Church in the early seventeenth century.

From our vantage point, in the course of a year the sun follows a curved path, called the ecliptic, through the sky. It can help to picture the ecliptic as a belt looped around the earth and projected into space. The sun's path is elliptical, so it lies at an angle to the equator. The size of this angle can change slightly, but at the moment it is approximately 23° 26'. This means that during the summer months the sun sits higher in the sky than it does during the winter.

For the purposes of astronomical measurement, the ecliptic is divided into twelve sections of 30° each, beginning with 0° Aries and ending with 29° Pisces. These twelve sections are the signs of the zodiac, and the astronomical year begins when the sun reaches 0° Aries at the spring equinox.

✎ What happens at the winter solstice ✎

The winter solstice occurs when the sun reaches its most southerly point in the sky. The sun is low in the sky at this time of year, even at noon when it always reaches its highest point in its daily motion, and the hours of daylight are at their shortest. In the northern hemisphere, the winter solstice occurs on or around 21 December (which is the summer solstice in the southern hemisphere). In the southern hemisphere, the winter solstice occurs on or around 21 June (which is the summer solstice in the northern hemisphere).

The exact moment of the winter solstice occurs when the sun reaches 0° Capricorn. This doesn't happen at the same time each year, which is why the winter solstice can occur at any point between 20, 21 and 22 December in the northern hemisphere. The darkest point of the year lasts for roughly four days, during which the sun stands still at its most southerly declination (the angle it forms with the celestial equator). It then begins to move northwards again.

The summer solstice occurs when the sun reaches 0° Cancer at some point between 20, 21 and 22 June in the northern hemisphere. The sun has reached its most northerly declination, and it stays there for four days before beginning to move southwards again.

☙ The four major astronomical ❧ points of the year

The year is divided into four major astronomical points, when the sun reaches a particular degree along the path of the ecliptic. The dates given are those that are most commonly recognised, although in practice they can vary slightly from year to year.

Date	Event	Sun's position	Sun's declination
21 March	Spring equinox	0° Aries	0° 0' N
21 June	Summer solstice	0° Cancer	23° 26' N
23 September	Autumn equinox	0° Libra	0° 0' S
21 December	Winter solstice	0° Capricorn	23° 26' S

FAST FOOD

The Christmas season can be an excuse for almost unbridled gluttony, often accompanied by a shrug and the inevitable words 'After all, it *is* Christmas'. And indeed it is.

There are so many temptations in the run-up to Christmas, ranging from the need to test out every brand of mince pie you can find to parties where it would be rude not to have double helpings of everything. And that's before we get to the big day itself when, according to some authorities, we can easily shovel down 7,000 calories of food with scarcely a thought. It's OK because we'll be starting our diet on New Year's Day, we tell ourselves. Or maybe we should wait until the Christmas cake is finished. Not to mention all those boxes of chocolates and the sticky liqueurs that are a bit sweet but too good to tip down the sink.

In the past, however, our pre-Christmas food was a very different proposition.

✎ The Advent fast ✎

The run-up to Christmas is known as Advent, from the Latin *adventus*, meaning 'coming', and refers to the coming of Christ into the world. In many of the western Churches, Advent begins on the fourth Sunday before Christmas Day (so it starts at some point between 27 November to 3 December) and ends on Christmas Eve. However, Advent was once a much longer season.

Between the sixth and ninth centuries, Advent began on 12 November and was observed by both the clergy and laity as a strict forty-day fast, often known as St Martin's Lent. As its name implies, it was taken as seriously as the forty-day Lenten fast that precedes Easter, and no meat was eaten. The fast was preceded by a day of feasting on 11 November, which is the feast day of St Martin of Tours and often known as Martinmas. In the ninth century, the forty-day fast gave way to a four-week fast that was broken on Christmas Day. This fast might have been shorter but it was still observed very carefully.

Further changes occurred in the twelfth century, when fasting was no longer imposed on everyone. Instead, each person was expected to limit their diet according to their conscience. Christmas Eve was kept as a very strict fast, with no meat, fish or eggs, before the great feast that was eaten on Christmas Day.

✎ A hard time ✎

The Advent fast was all very well for people who had plenty of food to choose from, such as fish, vegetable stews and soups, but it was a miserable and meagre time for those who pretty much had to eat whatever they could get, which might only be some roughly milled bread and beans saved from that year's harvest.

The arrival of Christmas Day, with the promise of being able to eat something substantial again, must have been very welcome.

St Stephen's Day frolics

Christmas Day is followed on 26 December by St Stephen's Day. St Stephen was the first Christian martyr (he was stoned to death in AD 34 or 35), so was honoured by being given the day immediately after Christmas Day.

His day was a busy one and attracted all sorts of traditional pastimes. Today, we are more likely to spend the day slumped in a comatose heap or complaining that there isn't anything worth watching on television, but our ancestors found plenty of ways to amuse themselves. After the sanctity of Christmas Day, St Stephen's Day was clearly a good excuse to let off some seasonal steam. Sometimes, they really let rip.

～ Holly beating ～

In the nineteenth century, Boxing Day was celebrated in a strange manner in Tenby in South Wales. Men and boys would take branches of holly and go 'holly beating', which involved running through the streets on the lookout for girls. Once the unsuspecting girls were found, the boys would whack them on the arms with the holly until they drew blood. Why? It seems hard to believe it was a courting ritual. Instead, it may have been the remnants of an ancient rite intended to drive out evil spirits through some form of scourging with a magical plant.

Nowadays, of course, these holly beaters would be rewarded with ASBOs all round.

≈ Horse bleeding ≈

It wasn't only young women in Wales who ended up with scars on St Stephen's Day. In medieval times, horses in Britain didn't escape unharmed either. Customs associated with horses were practised throughout Europe on St Stephen's Day. In many countries, these practices didn't involve any bloodshed at all, but it was different in Britain. Here, it was widely believed that the best way to ensure your horse would be in good health during the coming year was to bleed it on St Stephen's Day. In the sixteenth century, Thomas Tusser wrote about the practice in his book *Five Hundred Points of Good Husbandry*:

> Ere Christmas be passed,
> Let horse be lett blood,
> For many a purpose
> It doth them much good.
> The day of St Stephen
> Old fathers did use;
> If that do mislike thee,
> Some other day choose.

The St Stephen for whom 26 December is named had no connection with horses while he was alive, so why his feast day is now associated with horses is a matter of some debate. One theory is that his name has gradually been confused with the equine associations of another St Stephen. This Swedish saint, who may be mythological, was an early Christian missionary who loved horses.

❧ Hunting ❧

Hunting has been a popular sport in Britain for centuries, with quarries ranging in the past from deer and wild boar to hares and foxes. Today, the hunting with dogs of most animals is banned in England and Wales (although there are plans from some quarters to overturn the 2004 Hunting Act) and Scotland (where hunting was banned in 2002). However, drag hunting, in which dogs follow a scent laid by a runner, is legal. Many hunts have an annual meet on Boxing Day, which may be another example of the association between St Stephen's Day and horses.

❧ Law-abiding ❧

Members of Inner Temple in London – one of the four Inns of Court in which barristers have their chambers – once got up to lots of fun and games on St Stephen's Day. On one notable St Stephen's Day in Tudor times, the presiding Lord of Misrule let a cat and a fox into Inner Temple, where they were hunted with a pack of hounds until all that was left was a mess of blood and fur.

The members of Inner Temple clearly liked to enjoy themselves. They would get together on St Stephen's Day, drink plenty of alcohol, and sing,

> Bring hither the bowle
> The burning browne bowle,
> And quaff the rich juice right merrilie;
> Let the wise cup go round
> Till the solid ground
> Shall shake at the noise of our revelrie.

CHRISTMAS EVENTS

Christmas and the New Year are two major markers at the end of December, but the world doesn't stop because of the festivities. Here is a selection of some of the momentous British events that have occurred at this time of the year over the centuries.

25 DECEMBER 1066 Coronation of William I (known forever after as William the Conqueror) at Westminster Abbey

24 DECEMBER 1167 The future King John of England is born at Beaumont Palace, Oxford

24 DECEMBER 1430 Anne of Burgundy gives the Bedford Hours, an illuminated medieval prayer book that is now one of Britain's great literary treasures, as a Christmas present to her nine-year-old nephew, Henry VI. At the time, it was unusual to give Christmas gifts

24 DECEMBER 1515 Henry VIII appoints Thomas Wolsey as Lord Chancellor of England

1 JANUARY 1600 Scotland officially begins its year on 1 January instead of 25 March

25 DECEMBER 1642 Isaac Newton (who was knighted in 1705) is born in Woolsthorpe, Lincolnshire

1 JANUARY 1651 The exiled Charles II is crowned King of Scotland at Scone Abbey, Perthshire

1 JANUARY 1660 Samuel Pepys writes his first entry in his diary

31 DECEMBER 1695	A window tax is introduced in England, so householders have to pay tax on the number of windows in their properties
1 JANUARY 1766	James Edward Stuart, 'The Old Pretender' (to the English and Scottish thrones), dies in Rome
1 JANUARY 1772	The London Credit Exchange Company issues the world's first travellers' cheques
1 JANUARY 1788	The first issue of *The Times* newspaper is printed
1 JANUARY 1801	The Acts of Union come into force, in which the Kingdom of Great Britain (England and Scotland) is united with the Kingdom of Ireland to form the United Kingdom of Great Britain and Ireland. The Church of Ireland and the Church of England are also united to form the United Church of England and Ireland
25 DECEMBER 1871	Christmas Day becomes a bank holiday in Scotland
26 DECEMBER 1871	Boxing Day becomes a bank holiday in England, Wales and Northern Ireland
1 JANUARY 1872	New Year's Day becomes a bank holiday in Scotland
1 JANUARY 1881	The Post Office issues the world's first postal orders
1 JANUARY 1881	Dr John Watson meets Sherlock Holmes (the characters invented by Sir Arthur Conan Doyle) for the first time
24 DECEMBER 1914	The first aerial bomb is dropped on Britain when a German plane tries to bomb Dover Castle in the First World War

25 DECEMBER 1914	An unofficial Christmas truce is observed by British and German soldiers on the Western Front
31 DECEMBER 1923	The midnight chimes of Big Ben are recorded and broadcast live for the first time
1 JANUARY 1927	The British Broadcasting Company becomes the British Broadcasting Corporation, having been granted a royal charter
25 DECEMBER 1932	George V broadcasts the first Christmas Day radio message on the BBC
26 DECEMBER 1943	The German battleship *Scharnhorst* is sunk off Norway by HMS *Duke of York* during the Battle of North Cape in the Second World War
1 JANUARY 1948	Britain's railways are nationalised as British Railways
1 JANUARY 1951	The BBC broadcasts the first national episode of the radio drama *The Archers*
31 DECEMBER 1960	Call-ups for National Service formally end in the UK
31 DECEMBER 1960	The farthing ceases to be legal tender
31 DECEMBER 1964	Donald Campbell, in his speedboat *Bluebird*, breaks the world water speed record in Perth, Australia, by reaching an average speed of 444.71 km/h (276.33 mph)
24 DECEMBER 1965	A large meteorite lands in Barwell, Leicestershire
1 JANUARY 1970	The age of majority in the UK is reduced from 21 to 18

1 JANUARY 1973   Britain and Ireland join the EEC (European
                    Economic Community)

26 DECEMBER 1974   Boxing Day becomes a bank holiday in
                    Scotland

1 JANUARY 1975   New Year's Day becomes a bank holiday in
                    England, Wales and Northern Ireland

25 DECEMBER 2003   The British-built *Beagle 2* probe, which is
                    supposed to land on Mars on this day, fails to
                    keep the appointment and disappears

TIDINGS OF GREAT JOY

For unto us a child is born, unto us a son is given
... and his name shall be called Wonderful,
Counsellor, The mighty God, The everlasting
Father, The Prince of Peace.

ISAIAH 9:6-7

THE NATIVITY

The story of Jesus Christ's birth, over two thousand years ago, is known to billions of people around the world. It has been depicted in paintings, described in books, sung about in carols and hymns, and acted out in Nativity plays and many other dramas. As a result, we know the story inside out. Or so we think, until we turn to the relevant chapters of St Matthew and St Luke in the New Testament and discover that each of them focuses on different aspects of the Nativity. It is only by piecing together their two accounts that we arrive at the story we know today. What is most striking, though, is that one of the central details we now take for granted isn't mentioned at all.

≋ The Annunciation ≋

Christ's Nativity begins with what is called the Annunciation – the Angel Gabriel proclaiming to Mary that she would conceive a son called Jesus, but that it would be a virgin birth. Luke's Gospel goes into a lot of detail about the conversation between Mary and Gabriel, who tells her, 'The Holy Ghost shall come upon thee, and the power of the Highest shall overshadow thee; therefore also that holy thing which shall be born of thee shall be called the Son of God' (Luke 1:35).

At the time, Mary was 'espoused' to Joseph, a carpenter in Nazareth who was a descendant of the ruling House of David. While Luke tells us about Mary, Matthew's Gospel concentrates on Joseph's reaction to the news and how the 'angel of the Lord' visited Joseph to set his mind at rest by explaining the situation: 'Behold, a virgin shall be with child, and shall bring forth a son, and he shall be called Emmanuel, which being interpreted is, God with us' (Matthew 1:23).

∽ The journey to Bethlehem ∽

The second chapter of Luke tells us that Caesar Augustus decreed that 'all the world should be taxed' (Luke 2:1), so Mary and Joseph had to travel to Bethlehem in Judea 'because he was of the house and lineage of David' (2:4). Mary was heavily pregnant by now, and before long she had gone into labour. But Bethlehem was so crowded that there was nowhere for the couple to stay, so she gave birth to her child and 'laid him in a manger; because there was no room for them in the inn' (Luke 2:7).

∽ The story of the stable ∽

It is at this point that the story in the Bible differs so dramatically from the one that we know so well today. Although Luke tells us that Mary and Joseph couldn't find a bed for the night and so Mary laid Jesus in a manger (a small trough for cattle fodder), he makes no mention of where that manger was. It is commonly believed, because of the manger, that Jesus was born in a stable, but this information does not come from Luke. As for Matthew, he refers to 'a house' (Matthew 2:11). This means the Bible does not say that Jesus was born in a stable, even though that image has appeared in countless paintings and illustrations for centuries.

Many paintings of the Nativity show the Holy Family surrounded by animals, and in particular an ox and an ass. After all, they are obvious occupants of a stable. Although the Gospels don't describe an ox or ass being at the scene of Jesus's birth, these two animals have long been associated with the Nativity because of what is written in the Old Testament in Isaiah 1:3, 'The ox knoweth his owner, and the ass his master's crib: but Israel doth not know, my people doth not consider.'

According to historians, mangers were not kept inside stables at the time that Jesus was born. Instead, they were positioned on the sides of roads or in courtyards. Stables, as we know them, did not exist because the climate in Israel was mild enough for animals to be kept in the open air all year round. As for there not being any room 'in the inn', a more exact translation of the original Greek version of Luke's Gospel would be 'in the guestroom', implying that the Holy Family had come to stay with relatives. Perhaps the house was already full to bursting when Mary and Joseph arrived, so they had to make do with the courtyard.

∽ The wise men ∽

Matthew and Luke each describe a specific group of people coming to visit the infant Jesus. Matthew concentrates solely on what are now known as the Three Wise Men. However, he only mentions 'wise men from the east' (Matthew 2:1), and doesn't say how many there were. It was later assumed by the western Church that, because the wise men brought three gifts, there must have been three of them, and this idea has since taken root. In the eastern Church, however, it is thought that there were twelve wise men.

Matthew tells us that the wise men visited King Herod to ask him where they could find the child whose birth as the King of the Jews had been prophesied and who would 'rule my people Israel' (2:6). They knew he had been born because they could see the star that proclaimed his birth shining in the night sky. This news alarmed Herod, who told the wise men to go to Bethlehem, search out the child and 'bring me word again, that I may come and worship him also' (2:8).

The wise men were guided by the star to the place where Jesus was born, because it 'stood over where the young child was' (Matthew 2:9). When the wise men saw Mary and her baby, they presented the child with their gifts of gold, frankincense and myrrh. A dream warned them not to return to Herod with their news, so they returned home by a different route. Joseph also had an important dream, in which an angel told him to take his young family to Egypt, otherwise Herod would find the infant Jesus and kill him.

❧ The shepherds ❧

Luke's Gospel is silent on the subject of the wise men and concentrates instead on a group of shepherds who were 'abiding in the field, keeping watch over their flock by night' (Luke 2:8). They were visited by an angel who told them of the birth of 'a Saviour, which is Christ the Lord' (2:11), whom they would find 'wrapped in swaddling clothes, lying in a manger' (2:12). 'And suddenly there was with the angel a multitude of the heavenly host praising God and saying, "Glory to God in the highest, and on earth peace, good will toward men" (2:13). The shepherds went to Bethlehem to find the baby. As the angels had foretold, they found him in a manger and 'they made known abroad the saying which was told them concerning this child' (2:17).

❧ The massacre of the innocents ❧

Matthew's Gospel continues the story, which now becomes much darker. Herod waited for the return of the wise men. When they failed to materialise, he realised they had duped him and decided that the only way he could get rid of this newborn child who threatened his authority over Israel was to order the slaughter of all children under the age of two in Bethlehem. (This massacre is commemorated on 28 December as Holy Innocents' Day or Childermas.)

When Herod died, an angel appeared to Joseph in Egypt, telling him it was safe to take his family back to Israel. They settled in Nazareth, thereby fulfilling the prophesy that Christ 'shall be called a Nazarene' (Matthew 2:23). Both Matthew and Luke, and the other two Gospels of Mark and John, describe the rest of Jesus's life. Herod might have failed to kill him as a newborn baby, but Pontius Pilate succeeded when he was a man. This is the story that we remember each Easter, with both Easter and Christmas continuing to be the two major festivals of the Christian calendar.

IN SEARCH OF THE MAGI

According to the Gospel of St Matthew, the wise men (also known as the Magi) brought Jesus gifts of gold, frankincense and myrrh (2:11). This visit is called the Epiphany, the name of which comes from the Greek *epiphanein*, meaning 'to manifest'; in biblical terms it means the manifestation of Christ, as the son of God, to the

Gentiles (non-Jews). In this case, the Gentiles were the Magi. The western Christian Church celebrates Epiphany on 6 January.

❧ Who were the Magi? ❧

The Gospels of St Matthew and St Luke both describe the story of the Nativity, but only Matthew mentions the wise men and does not specify how many were involved.

The Bible is also silent on exactly who these wise men were. They were deemed to have been kings, possibly because Psalms 72:11 says 'all kings shall fall down before him'. Yet there is also a theory that they were Zoroastrian astrologers, hence their interest in the brilliant star that guided them to Jesus's birthplace. (In those days, astrology was a respected science and wasn't regarded with the scepticism that it frequently receives today.)

In the eighth century, a chronicle that may have been written in Egypt, called *Excerpta Latina Barberi*, gave the names of the three Magi as Bithisarea, Melichior and Gathaspa. These were eventually translated by the western Church as Balthazar from Arabia, Melchior from Persia and Gasper (or Casper) from India.

❧ The gifts of the Magi ❧

We are told that the Magi brought gifts of gold, frankincense and myrrh. These have a practical application but they also carry a deep spiritual significance. We will never know whether this significance was intended by the Magi or whether it is simply the result of centuries of Christian scholarship, analysis and interpretation.

Gold is an excellent gift for a newborn child, assuming that you can afford it. After all, many godparents give their new godchildren money in one form or another. Perhaps the Magi suspected that the parents of the child they were searching for might welcome some ready cash. Gold is, of course, a precious metal but it was also valued for its medicinal qualities long before Jesus was born. It was considered to be purifying, which would have been very useful at a time when many women and their babies died from infection during or after childbirth. In terms of gold's spiritual significance, it is a suitable gift for a king, and would have symbolised Christ's position as King of the Jews.

Frankincense (*Boswellia* spp.), which is an aromatic resin, was also a valuable medicine at the time of Jesus's birth. It staunches the flow of blood, heals wounds and is useful in treating uterine conditions, so it would have been highly appropriate for use in childbirth. When burnt it purifies the air, calms nervous tension and can induce a meditative state, so it is also an important ingredient of incense. Therefore, its spiritual significance might be that Christ is a deity to whom one prays.

Myrrh (*Commiphora* spp.) is another aromatic gum whose medicinal properties were first discovered thousands of years ago in the east. It is particularly useful as an analgesic and for cleaning wounds, so would have been a most practical gift for a woman who has just given birth in difficult circumstances. It is also a perfume, so could have been used to mask any unpleasant smells. But myrrh had a more sombre use, too, because it was used in embalming and for anointing the dead. In terms of its significance, it is therefore the darkest of the three gifts, because it was a reminder of Christ's mortality, foreshadowing his eventual crucifixion and death.

SING, CHOIRS OF ANGELS

Angels play a central role in the Bible's story of the birth of Jesus. They act as messengers, telling Mary that she was going to bear a child (Luke 1:26-35), informing Joseph of the momentous news while he slept (Matthew 1:20-25) and announcing the birth of the baby Jesus to the shepherds in the fields (Luke 2:8-15).

In the King James Bible, these angels are generally described as 'angels of the Lord', although occasionally they are given specific names. They appear in many other sections of the Bible as well, of course. Several medieval writers wanted to know more because lumping them into one category of 'angels of the Lord' was unsatisfying. Using the Bible as their primary source, and using some of the apocryphal Gospels that were not included in the Bible, they devised a list of the different realms of angels.

St Thomas Aquinas, whose thirteenth-century musings on angels were inspired by the writings of theologian Pseudo-Dionysius in the fifth and sixth centuries, created a hierarchy of angels that we still refer to today. Aquinas divided the angelic realms into nine sections, which he called 'choirs', starting with the choir that has the closest proximity to God. Each choir plays a particular role in Heaven. Some of the Bible's descriptions of these angels are remarkable.

SERAPHIM	Also known as 'the burning ones' because they are alight with divine love, they guard God's throne.
CHERUBIM	They protect entrances, and have wings, large animal bodies and the faces of humans or lions.
THRONES	These angels administer justice on God's behalf. They have human bodies with four faces, and move around on wheels covered with eyes.
DOMINIONS	These are the angels that take care of the countries of the world. They carry sceptres and swords.
VIRTUES	Virtues are allowed to change the physical laws of the universe, but only when it's absolutely vital to do so. They bestow faith and courage on humans.
POWERS	This choir of angels includes the angels that protect us during birth and death. They continually battle against the forces of evil.

PRINCIPALITIES These angels guard the world's many religions and their sacred places. They also keep a watchful eye over the world's rulers.

ARCHANGELS These are the angels, such as Gabriel, that convey God's messages to humans. Each of them has a male and a female aspect.

ANGELS Angels work directly with humans, helping and protecting us. This choir includes the guardian angels who watch over us throughout our lives.

THE STAR OF BETHLEHEM

St Matthew's Gospel tells us that the Magi, or Three Wise Men, were guided to the infant Jesus by a star that not only shone above his birthplace but 'stood over where the young child was' (2:9). They saw the star twice – before their journey began (2:2) and when they finally found the baby Jesus (2:9). Before they found Jesus they visited Herod to ask him for directions, but it is clear that he knew nothing about 'the star in the east' that the Magi had seen. This suggests that the star was easily seen by those who were familiar with the night sky (and the Magi are believed to have been astrologers), but was not so startling that absolutely everyone couldn't help noticing it.

What could this remarkable astronomical event have been? Was it a star, a comet or a planet? Or was it purely symbolic and not real at all?

❧ Artistic licence ❧

Some medieval artists who painted glorious depictions of the Nativity were quite inventive on the subject of the Star of Bethlehem. 'Adoration of the Magi', a fresco painted in 1304 by Giotto di Bondone, shows a comet swooping across the sky above the stable in which Jesus lies. (Giotto had seen what we now know as Halley's Comet in 1301 and was profoundly affected by the experience. Rather wonderfully, when the European Space Agency launched a robotic spacecraft to study the comet in 1986, it was called *Giotto* in his honour.) Other painters had different interpretations of the Star of Bethlehem. In Domenico Ghirlandaio's 1488 painting, also called 'Adoration of the Magi', a huge and radiant star hangs above four angels.

❧ Historical facts ❧

Clearly, no one was certain about the exact nature of the Star of Bethlehem. We might have a better idea of this if we could identify the time frame in which we're searching, and then look for notable astronomical phenomena during that time. We don't know exactly when Jesus was born (although many historians believe it was no later than 6 BC) but, if the Bible is correct, we know that Herod was alive at the time because he ordered the death of every child below the age of two in the hope that this would include the newborn 'King of the Jews', as the Magi called Jesus (Matthew 2:2). This should help to narrow down the options but, unhelpfully, there are two theories about the date of Herod's death. One is that he died in March or April 6 BC, and another is that he died in 1 BC.

One important clue when searching for remarkable astronomical events during this period is that the Three Wise Men saw the star twice. If astronomers could identify the exact celestial event, they would know when Jesus was born, so it is quite understandable that this puzzle has occupied scientists for centuries.

≈ Was it a supernova? ≈

Stars occupy what appear to us to be fixed positions in the sky, so they can't move at dramatic speed across the sky in order to settle over a specific site. They also are unlikely, in the normal course of events, to suddenly become so bright that they stand out in an unusual fashion. However, a supernova (exploding star) might possibly fulfil these criteria. Chinese astronomers at the time kept detailed records of what was happening in the skies, and recorded a series of novae in 5 and 4 BC. Is this what the Magi saw? Yet surely if the supernova was unnaturally bright, other people – including Herod – would have seen it as well.

≈ Was it a comet? ≈

One theory is that the Star of Bethlehem wasn't a star at all but a comet (a frozen lump of rock and dust), as depicted in Giotto's painting. Perhaps it was the comet that was later identified as Halley's Comet? After all, this comet can be seen with the naked eye, has an orbit of roughly 76 years and its motion has been tracked since 240 BC. One argument against the star being a comet is that comets have always been regarded as omens of disaster, usually presaging war or the death of a king, so it was unlikely to have been considered to bring good news.

≈ Was it a planet? ≈

The word 'planet' comes from the Greek *planetes*, meaning 'wanderer', because planets have a discernible orbit through the sky, so this is the celestial candidate that is most likely to have been the Star of Bethlehem. But which planet, and what made it so notable?

A planet can appear brighter than usual for several reasons, such as when it's nearer the earth than normal and therefore looks larger. It can also appear brighter to the naked eye because what looks like a single planet might actually be an alignment of two or more planetary bodies, separated by vast tracts of space, but appearing to be next to each other from our perspective on earth. This is called a conjunction.

Planetary conjunctions happen frequently, so this conjunction must have been very special – and visible – to merit so much attention from the Magi. Because the Magi saw it twice, it would have to be a conjunction that was repeated at least once. This happens because planets can appear to move backwards (known as retrograde motion) as well as forwards, so they seem to double back on themselves before eventually turning to direct motion again. They can do this more than once and if they are travelling at roughly the same speed they will form more than one conjunction.

Are there any likely candidates? There was a triple conjunction (meaning a series of three conjunctions) of Jupiter and Saturn between 7 and 6 BC, and in 7 BC the two planets rose in the east close to the sun. Jupiter and Saturn form a conjunction every twenty years, so their meeting on this occasion would have had to be special in some way. In 2 BC, Venus and Jupiter formed their annual conjunction, but it was particularly bright because the planets appeared to be so close together. In fact, Venus was passing in front of Jupiter to form a partial occultation, and they were also positioned close to Regulus, which has long been considered the 'royal' star (it is in the constellation of Leo) and is one of the brightest stars in the night sky. Was this what drew the Magi to Bethlehem?

~ Was it symbolic? ~

Another theory is that the star never existed but is purely symbolic. For those who don't believe that Jesus ever lived, or who refute much of the contents of the Bible, this may be the most logical answer. For those who do believe in Jesus, this may be a deeply unsatisfactory conclusion.

Ultimately, perhaps it is up to each of us to make up our own minds about the explanation for the Star of Bethlehem, whether we regard it as a real astronomical event that was seen by others, something that was visible only to the Magi or simply one of the many examples of the mystery and poetry contained within the Bible.

THE FIRST NATIVITY SCENE

We might imagine that bemoaning the commercialisation of Christmas, with its emphasis on materialism through lavish gifts and its loss of spiritual meaning, is a very contemporary state of affairs. But we would be wrong. Even in the thirteenth century, there was concern about the approach that some people took to Christmas.

❧ The role of St Francis ❧

In 1223, Francis of Assisi (he was made a saint after his death), who was a church deacon, wanted to bring the Christmas message alive. He was concerned that people didn't understand it or were lacking in wonder about what had happened on that night in Bethlehem, and what it meant for mankind. That Christmas, he was visiting Greccio in Italy, and decided to recreate the Christmas story at that year's Midnight Mass, so everyone could experience it for themselves. Having received permission from the Pope, Honorius III, Francis created a living tableau of the Nativity in a cave near Greccio. He brought an ox and an ass, and filled a manger with hay.

The stories about this first Nativity scene differ, with some saying that Mary and Joseph were represented and others saying that the scene only contained animals. However, there was no baby lying in the manger. Yet it was said that while Francis preached to the congregation, his friend, John of Greccio, looked into the manger and saw a baby, which he believed to be a manifestation of the infant Jesus. A series of miracles that occurred afterwards, involving the hay that had been placed in the manger, were taken as confirmation that Christ had indeed materialised at that Mass. Women who were struggling with long labours were able to give birth easily when a few strands of hay were placed on top of them, and ailing local cattle were cured of long-standing illnesses when given the hay to eat.

The spot where this first Nativity scene was acted out is said to be marked by the Franciscan Sanctuary of Greccio.

❧ The development of Nativity scenes ❧

Word soon spread about this special Nativity tableau and it has been re-enacted in many Christian countries ever since.

By the end of the thirteenth century, static Nativity scenes were being crafted from a variety of materials, including wood, marble and pottery. And they continue to be popular today, frequently combining the Wise Men mentioned in St Matthew's Gospel with the shepherds and angels mentioned in St Luke's.

In many junior and primary schools, children celebrate the start of Christmas with nativity plays. Not only do these combine the characters from the two Gospels but they sometimes feature an entire menagerie of animals that receive no mention at all in the Bible. Would St Francis have approved? Let's hope so.

Ho, Ho, Ho!

I heard him exclaim, ere he drove out of sight,
'Happy Christmas to all, and to all a good-night!'

'A VISIT FROM ST NICHOLAS', CLEMENT C MOORE

THE ORIGINS OF FATHER CHRISTMAS

Father Christmas is an integral part of the secular aspect of Christmas for many of us, and particularly for children (regardless of their actual age). Christmas wouldn't be the same without him. He has a long and complex history, and he has been part of the midwinter festivities for centuries, even when he's been known by a very different name.

∾ The old gods ∾

One of the fascinating elements of folklore and mythology is seeing the crossover of stories between different cultures, and how invaders brought their own beliefs with them. Wotan was one of the gods of the ancient Teutonic tribes in pre-Christian times. He was said to ride across the sky in the Wild Hunt – a terrifying race that often included the souls of the dead and was thought to presage a disaster of some kind.

Odin was Wotan's counterpart in Old Norse mythology, which flourished in Scandinavia before it began to convert to Christianity in the eighth century. Odin had a long beard and was often depicted wearing a flowing cloak. He was the principal god of the Norse pantheon and was associated with warfare as well as magic. He was said to ride the sky on an eight-legged horse called Sleipnir, whose teeth bore carvings of the runes that Odin had discovered when he hung upside down from Yggdrasil, the Tree of Life. With the help of Sleipnir, Odin was said to place gifts in the shoes of any children who left out food for his flying horse.

Woden (also spelt Wodan) was the Anglo-Saxon equivalent of Odin. He was considered an important god until he was swept away by the spread of Christianity across Britain in the eighth century.

Did the stories surrounding this trio of ancient gods contribute to our beliefs about Father Christmas? We may never know for certain, but there are distinct and intriguing similarities.

THE STORY OF ST NICK

Have you ever wondered why it's traditional to put a bag of chocolate coins, wrapped in gold and silver foil, in children's Christmas stockings? It's all thanks to the legend surrounding St Nicholas, whose feast day is celebrated each 6 December.

Nicholas was the Bishop of Myra, in modern Turkey, in the fourth century. Many of the legends about Nicholas involve him saving the lives, or taking pity on, groups of three people who were either in peril or who suffered the most dreadful fate. One of these tales is especially grisly. The story is that during a severe famine St Nicholas discovered a butcher who had murdered three small boys and put their corpses in a barrel. The butcher planned to cure their bodies and sell them as succulent hams. St Nicholas was able to bring the three boys back to life, purely through the power of prayer, and release them. What he did to the butcher is not recorded.

Perhaps the most celebrated story about St Nicholas is that he once saved the virtue of three sisters whose father had fallen on desperately hard times. The father decided that his only option was to turn all three daughters into prostitutes. When St Nicholas heard about this, he was so horrified that he wrapped some gold coins in a piece of fabric and threw them into the man's house. The penniless father was thrilled and used the money to marry each of his daughters to her respective beloved. Some stories say that St Nicholas lobbed the money in through the man's open window. Another version is much more picturesque and has a direct bearing on several of our contemporary Christmas traditions. In this story, St Nicholas, who was clearly very modest about being such a compassionate benefactor, dropped a bag of coins down the family's chimney. The coins fell into the stockings that one of the daughters had washed and hung by the chimney to dry.

The legend of St Nicholas is still remembered across the world, but particularly in Europe. He goes by many names, according to the country concerned. For instance, he is San Nicola in Italy and St Nicolas in France, but perhaps the name that gives us the greatest clue about the impact his story has had on our traditional Christmas celebrations is the one by which he's known in Belgium and the Netherlands. Here, he is called Sinterklaas. The Anglicised version of this is, of course, Santa Claus.

THE TRIALS AND TRIBULATIONS OF CHRISTMAS

Christmas is such an established celebration now, with Father Christmas at its secular centre in Britain, that it is tempting to take them both for granted. But the development of Father Christmas and the accompanying festival has gone in fits and starts, and hasn't been nearly as smooth or easy as we might think.

The personification of Christmas

Many European countries developed traditions that revolved around St Nicholas and concerned him leaving gifts for children each 6 December. Things were different in Britain, however. The infant Christ was obviously an integral part of the festivities ('Christmas' translates as 'Christ's Mass'), but gradually another figure began to appear.

To date, the earliest recorded reference to Christmas as a person, rather than as a general festival, appears in the carol 'Sir Christèmas', which is attributed to Richard Smart, who was the rector of Plymtree in Devon in 1435–77. The carol consists of a conversation between Sir Christèmas and some people who welcome him.

Christmas was also sometimes represented as a person during the sixteenth and seventeenth centuries, when the festivities in aristocratic circles were presided over by the Lord of Misrule. He called himself such names as 'Prince Christmas' or 'Captain Christmas'. A figure associated with Christmas also appeared in mummers' plays, often dressed in a brown or green hooded robe. But he was thin at this point: his girth grew much later.

∼ Christmas turns political ∼

In December 1616, James I and the rest of the English court watched a seasonal masque (an elaborate entertainment consisting of singing, dancing and acting) written by Ben Jonson. It was called *Christmas, His Masque*, and featured a cast of suitably festive characters with such names (using the original spellings) as Minc'd-Pie, Caroll, Mis-Rule and New-Yeares-Gift. The main character, however, was none other than Christmas. As well as being a way to entertain the court, the masque was making a political point about the severe restrictions that the Puritan faction of the Protestant Reformation was placing on Christmas celebrations. Christmas had already been excised from the Scots calendar on the grounds that it was a Papist Mass and not mentioned in the Bible. It experienced a similar fate in England in 1647, where the law wasn't revoked until 1660.

The character of Christmas ('an old reverend gentleman in furred gown and cap') made another political appearance in 1638, in Thomas Nabbe's play *The Spring's Glorie*. He has an argument with a character called Shrovetide, who tells him he's 'past date, you are out of the Almanack'. Father Christmas was at the centre of several other plays, as well as pamphlets, that defended him against the war of attrition being mounted on him by the Puritans.

The Victorian Father Christmas

Even after Christmas was reinstated as a festival in 1660, it had a much lower profile in the following years. Things got even worse with the arrival of another foe – the Industrial Revolution, which lasted from the mid 1700s to the mid 1800s. The transition from rural to urban employment separated families as workers moved into towns in order to get employment, and the new manufacturing industries saw people working very hard for very long hours. Christmas suffered, as a result. For many people, it was as though the heart had gone out of it.

But not everyone was prepared for this state of affairs to continue. A group of writers and illustrators was determined to revive Christmas. They wanted the celebration to return to what they saw as the good old days when scattered families and friends were reunited each December to enjoy a traditional festive season. They yearned for a time when young and old gathered round the hearth, people told stories, enmities were forgotten and everyone remembered what was most important to them: each other. It's fair to say they succeeded!

One unexpected offshoot of this was the establishment of Father Christmas as a solid (literally as well as figuratively) and recognisable character. He gradually changed from being the slim, slightly mysterious character of old and became fat and jolly. The original John Leech illustration of the Ghost of Christmas Present in Charles Dickens's *A Christmas Carol* was tremendously influential. Dickens described this ghost as 'a jolly Giant, glorious to see', with his cheerful face, fur-trimmed coat (which was green) and a holly wreath set upon his brown curly hair, not to mention the mounds of delicious food that surrounded him. This was more like it! Here was a Father Christmas that everyone could welcome into their homes and hearts.

The images of Father Christmas began to change. He kept his hooded gown but it gradually altered in colour, switching from green or brown to the red we know today. By the late 1800s, thanks to the influence of Santa Claus in the United States and St Nicholas in mainland Europe, the British Father Christmas was the bearer of gifts, too. Children hung up their stockings on Christmas Eve, either on the ends of their beds or by the sitting room fireplace, in the hope that Father Christmas would arrive in the night and fill those stockings with presents.

The commercialisation of Father Christmas

By the early twentieth century, images of Father Christmas were being used for advertising. What's more, the newly emerging department stores discovered that having a resident Father Christmas was a massive draw for thousands of small children who would whisper their Christmas requests into his ear and then be given a present, often in return for a discreet payment by their parents.

And so it goes on today. Smaller children queuing to meet Father Christmas in shops are often stunned into silence at the thought that they are meeting the real McCoy. Older children may question if he really is Father Christmas, and are often told that he's a representative of the true Father Christmas who, of course, can't be there because he's busy at the North Pole supervising all the preparations for his official arrival on Christmas Eve.

ON SANTA'S TRAIL

It is often assumed that Father Christmas and Santa Claus are the same person, or that Father Christmas is the old-fashioned name for the more modern and Americanised Santa Claus. But that isn't the case at all. Historically, they are two very different figures, even if the legends surrounding them have now become confused. Here is one theory about how the American Santa got his name.

∞ Sinterklaas ∞

The story of St Nicholas, the fourth-century Turkish bishop whose feast day is 6 December, had a huge bearing on the development of Father Christmas. St Nicholas goes by many names, according to the language of the country in which he is being honoured. In the Netherlands and Belgium he is known as Sinterklaas, which is a very similar name to that of Santa Claus.

When Europeans began to emigrate to America, from the seventeenth century, they took their beliefs and traditions with them. New York was originally a Dutch colonial settlement called New

Amsterdam, and the children of the Dutch settlers would undoubtedly have unwrapped the gifts left by Sinterklaas when they woke
on the morning of 6 December.

Sinterklaas is not the only Christmas figure to have been imported
to the United States with the continued influx of Europeans, but his
name tells us that he was highly influential in the development of
Santa Claus's own name. But a different Christmas figure influenced
the night on which Santa Claus busily delivered gifts to children.

∽ Christkind ∽

The Protestant Reformation of the sixteenth and seventeenth centuries,
which had such a profound influence on the way we celebrate
Christmas, affected most of Europe. Strict Protestants believed that St
Nicholas, in his many guises, was no longer considered to be a suitable
figure to visit children because he was a saint and therefore part of the
Roman Catholic religion that was now being so vociferously renounced.
St Nicholas was replaced by a blond-haired, angelic-looking child who
was a representative of the infant Jesus. In Germany, his name was
Christkind (and sometimes Christkindl), which translates as
'Christchild'. Children expecting him to arrive on the night of 5–6
December were disappointed, because he only appeared during the
night of 24–25 December, in honour of Christ's birth.

As with Sinterklaas, the traditions surrounding the Christkind
accompanied those European settlers who believed in him when
they emigrated to America. Eventually, the Christkind's name was
Americanised to Kriss Kringle – one of the names by which Santa
Claus is still known in the United States.

∽ The arrival of Santa Claus ∽

At some point in the nineteenth century, the distinctions between the
figures and names of St Nicholas and the Christkind (not to mention
British traditions surrounding Father Christmas) became so blurred
that they coalesced into the character we now know as Santa Claus.

Illustrations of the new Santa, with his chubby tummy and sack full of toys, began to appear in American books and magazines in the mid-nineteenth century. Such was his popularity that he was quickly being used for political purposes – in January 1863, during the height of the American Civil War, the popular magazine *Harper's Weekly* showed him addressing a rally while wearing the American flag and sitting on his sleigh. The illustrator was Thomas Nast, whose depictions of Santa Claus had a profound and widespread impact on Santa's subsequent image.

It's a popular myth that Santa Claus gained his red and white outfit when Coca-Cola used him to advertise its soft drinks in the 1930s because he had been depicted in what are now his trademark colours long before then.

◈ Santa Claus today ◈

The character of Santa Claus has appeared in numerous films, cartoons, comic strips, books and songs, and this shows no sign of stopping. It looks as though he is here to stay.

Or should that be here to 'sleigh'?

STOCKING UP FOR CHRISTMAS

When you are a child, hanging up your stocking on Christmas Eve means that the interminable waiting and uncharacteristic good behaviour is finally, blessedly, over. All you have to do now, if humanly possible, is to fall asleep, knowing that you will wake on Christmas morning, ready to open a bulging stocking full of presents.

It is difficult to say exactly when Christmas stockings first became such an important feature of the festivities in Britain. The earliest known mention of any Christmas stocking comes in the poem *A Visit from St Nicholas*, which is credited to Clement C Moore (although it is not certain if he actually wrote it himself, as it may have been written by a man called Henry Livingston and then 'borrowed' by Moore) and was first published in America in 1823. And the image conjured up is one that has stayed in our collective memory ever since:

The stockings were hung by the chimney with care
In the hopes that St Nicholas soon would be there.

It's enough to make you want to buy a house with a huge traditional fireplace, simply so you can decorate it with Victorian-themed stockings in happy anticipation on Christmas Eve.

❧ The story behind the stocking ❧

This tradition of Christmas stockings comes from Europe and is much older than Moore's poem. Odin and Sleipnir, his flying horse, and also St Nicholas, have all played their part in what became the practice of putting Christmas gifts in stockings. And it was a practice that soon caught on. In 1854, a children's book called *Carl Krinken or The Christmas Stocking*, written by Susan Warner, was published in America and Britain. It told the story of a small boy whose parents were very poor, and who received a magical Christmas stocking full of presents that could talk. In 1884, a story called 'Santa Claus and All His Works', by George Webster, featured a drawing by Thomas Nast, a German-born illustrator working in America. The illustration shows Santa Claus unloading his sack full of toys in front of a fireplace while a little girl watches from her bed. Four stockings hang from the chimney breast, but they must be there for decoration because they are clearly much too small to hold Santa's gifts.

Stockings soon appeared by British fireplaces as well as American ones, although British children looked forward to the gifts left by Father Christmas rather than Santa Claus. At some point the traditional stocking – often a long sock – gave way in many homes to a pillowcase. What this lacks in tradition it more than makes up for in the number of presents it can contain.

❧ Writing to Father Christmas ❧

But how did the children tell Father Christmas or Santa Claus what they wanted him to bring them? One tried and tested way was – and still is – dictated by logic. If Father Christmas comes down the chimney on Christmas Eve to deliver presents, it makes sense to post a letter to him up that same chimney. Somehow, the children know he will receive it. Another option is for children to give their letter to their parents, so they can sort out the tricky business of getting it to Father Christmas. In Britain, children can also get in touch with Father Christmas by writing to him at a special address supplied each year by the Royal Mail.

❧ That magical feeling ❧

Millions of children have woken early on Christmas morning and inched their feet down their bed in the pre-dawn silence until they find their stocking – heavy (with luck), enticingly lumpy and, most of all, full of promise. In the past, stocking presents might be simple, such as a tangerine, a bag of chocolate coins, some toys and the annual of a favourite comic or television programme. Today, the presents might be more sophisticated and vastly more expensive. But for many children, both young and old, waking up to their stocking on Christmas morning is still the most magical part of a magical day.

RUDOLPH AND CO

When little children lie awake on Christmas Eve, too excited to sleep and with their ears cocked for the sound of you-know-who's sleigh landing on the roof, they may have hospitably put out some food and drink for the visitors. A glass of milk or a mug of cocoa, perhaps, for Father Christmas himself, and some choice carrots for his team of reindeer. But that raises an interesting question. Exactly how many reindeer does Father Christmas have? It would be terrible if there weren't enough carrots to go round.

According to *A Visit from St Nicholas*, there are eight reindeer, each of which has a name. This is the order in which they are listed in the poem:

> Dasher
> Dancer
> Prancer
> Vixen
> Comet
> Cupid
> Donner
> Blitzen

The names of the first six are easy and haven't changed since the poem was first published anonymously in 1823. But Donner and Blitzen are a different matter. Their names are the German for thunder and lightning. Originally, Donner was Dunder and Blitzen was Blixem (the Dutch words for thunder and lightning). A later version of the poem, published in 1837, changed the reindeer's names to Donder and Blixen. They changed again, at some later point, to their current forms of Donner and Blitzen.

But what about Rudolph? Isn't he the chief reindeer, thanks to his red nose that glows so brightly and enables Father Christmas to see his way in the dark? In contrast with Dasher, Dancer and Co, Rudolph is a relatively recent addition to the team. He was created by Robert L May, who was an advertising copywriter, and first appeared in a colouring book, called *Rudolph the Red-nosed Reindeer*, in America in 1939. Rudolph went on to become the subject of a song, further books and a film.

What his fellow reindeer think of Rudolph's worldwide status is not known because, unlike many other celebrities, they never give interviews.

In Our Fathers' Footsteps

A Christmas gambol oft could cheer
The poor man's heart through half the year.

'MARMION', SIR WALTER SCOTT

BOY BISHOPS

In medieval times, the season of Christmas was traditionally an opportunity to reverse the natural order of authority for a short while, so that servants became masters and vice versa. This happened in many ways, and it even occurred in the Church.

❧ Electing the boy bishop ❧

The tradition of reversing the clerical pecking order probably began in Germany but was very popular in England for several centuries, beginning in the fourteenth century, if not earlier. At some point during December a young boy – usually a chorister from a cathedral school – would be elected by his fellow choristers as the temporary bishop of the diocese over Christmas. This young man (and it was always a young man, never a young woman – such a thing was unthinkable at the time) was called the boy bishop and would carry out almost all of the bishop's duties, other than saying Mass. The boy bishop was allowed to travel around the diocese, could boss the other choristers about, declare holidays (which must have ensured his popularity) and generally had the sort of good time that was strictly off limits during the rest of the year.

The exact details of the election of a boy bishop varied from one diocese to another. Sometimes the boy bishop for the year was chosen on St Nicholas's Day (6 December), which is traditionally associated with children. He would keep his elevated post until Holy Innocents' Day (28 December), which is also associated with children but in a much less jolly way. In other dioceses, the boy bishop only ruled during St Nicholas's Day or during Holy Innocents' Day itself.

❧ The boy bishop's duties ❧

The boy bishop would attend cathedral services in full fig, complete with a bishop's mitre and crozier, and his fellow choristers would also wear ceremonial robes and parade around the cathedral. The boy bishop and the real bishop swapped positions during the singing of the Magnificat, at the words 'he hath put down the mighty from their seat'. The boy bishop would preach the sermon, although it was always written for him, as presumably it was considered far too risky to let him say whatever he pleased. Later in the service, he would bless the congregation in the part of the service known as the Blessing of the People, and might even be allowed to keep the money collected during the offering.

This was a very exciting event for everyone, choristers and congregation alike, and the cathedrals were packed while the boy bishop was in charge. An added benefit for him was that he could look forward to a lavish ceremonial feast at some point during Christmas. Most adolescent boys are always hungry, but these choristers were even more likely to be in need of food because they weren't always fed very generously during the rest of the year.

The boy bishop at St Paul's Cathedral used to lead a procession through London in which the city was blessed, and this practice was adopted in other cities as well.

❧ In memoriam ❧

Happily, the boy bishop usually survived his period of election, but the medieval period was a time of high mortality rates. If a boy bishop died while in office, he was buried with full ceremony as though he were a real bishop. There is a tomb for one such boy bishop in the north aisle of the nave of Salisbury Cathedral.

∞ Banned! ∞

The practice of electing a boy bishop each December became so popular that it spread from cathedrals and was eventually a feature of any church that could boast its own choir. The service in which clergy and choristers changed places also grew a good deal more rowdy as the years progressed, with the clergy becoming as boisterous as the choristers.

It is often said that all good things must come to an end, and so it was with the custom of boy bishops. Henry VIII was the first monarch to call a halt to the tradition in 1541 when the Protestant Reformation was gathering pace in Britain. He protested that the idea of boy bishops (being an example of 'vaine superstition') damaged the dignity of the Church and detracted from the proper business of worship. As Henry was now the head of the Church of England, he would have been acutely aware that the topsy-turvy tradition of boy bishops might have reflected badly on himself. In November 1554, Henry's daughter, Mary I (a devout Roman Catholic), revived the custom (which had originally been practised in Roman Catholic churches), although, rather confusingly, it was outlawed again the following month. Not that anyone took much notice, because they carried on as if the counter-order had never been issued. Even so, after Mary died her Protestant half-sister, Elizabeth I, clarified matters by abolishing the custom again.

∞ Revived! ∞

In recent years, the tradition of boy bishops has been revived, albeit with revisions, not only in England (including Hereford, Salisbury and Westminster cathedrals and many parish churches) but in other parts of Europe. And equal opportunities means that girl bishops can now be elected as well as boy bishops. What Henry VIII would have thought of that is anyone's guess.

COMPLIMENTS OF THE SEASON

Next time you are working your way through a huge pile of Christmas cards and trying to think of a charming and original message to write in each one while avoiding anything along the predictable lines of 'We *must* meet next year!', you might spare a thought for Sir Henry Cole. Whether you send him a charitable thought or something that might have come from the unreformed Scrooge is entirely between you and your conscience.

◈ Special Christmas cards ◈

Sir Henry Cole was a Victorian businessman and inventor who was responsible for the development of several things that we now take for granted. These include Christmas cards. Until the 1840s, some people liked to send cards to their family and friends at the New Year but Christmas wasn't marked in the same way. All that changed in 1843. That year (which, interestingly enough, is also the year when Charles Dickens published *A Christmas Carol*), Sir Henry hit on the idea of sending specially designed cards that would not only wish his recipients the compliments of the season but remind them of the miserable plight of the poor.

He commissioned John Callcott Horsley RA to design a card that combined these twin messages. The central panel showed a happy family celebrating Christmas. It was flanked on either side by smaller panels depicting kindly souls ministering to the poor. Sir Henry wrote the name of the recipient at the top of the card and signed his name at the bottom. The printed message read 'A Merry Christmas and a Happy New Year to You'.

∾ Commercial production ∾

This was a private undertaking, but the cards were obviously a success because in 1846 they went into commercial production. Felix Summerly's Home Treasury Office (a company that was owned by Sir Henry Cole), of Old Bond Street, London, issued 1,000 cards bearing the original design. They sold for one shilling (5 pence in today's currency) each.

Alas, not everyone approved. Eagle-eyed custodians of public morals noticed that slap bang in the middle of the central panel was a small girl drinking something alcoholic from her doting mother's glass. This wasn't the invitation to early vice that it might seem today, since many Victorian children were given alcohol to drink at parties, but it still offended some people, who levelled accusations of the card 'fostering the moral corruption of young children'.

∾ The second Christmas card ∾

In 1848, a young artist called William Maw Egley produced what is believed to be the second British Christmas card. It was an etching, showing cheerful Christmas celebrations along the top of the card. By contrast, the bottom of the card showed scenes of impoverished misery, presumably as a reminder that Christmas is a time to remember those less fortunate than ourselves.

∾ Hearts and flowers ∾

The custom of sending the cards soon began to grow. It was perfectly suited to Victorian sentiments, and especially to the language of flowers. As a result, many young lovers were able to exchange cards that appeared innocent enough to pass muster on the family mantelpiece, even though the flowers adorning them spoke in code of fevered and heartfelt passions that would have set Papa's mutton-chop whiskers quivering with paternal displeasure.

Young lovers could also be inventive when sticking on the postage stamp: a stamp that lies on its side, with the image pointing to the left, means 'I am longing to see you'. Receiving such a message would have delighted many a Victorian lover, while their parents remained in blissful ignorance.

POST EARLY FOR CHRISTMAS

You might imagine that the production of the first commercial Christmas cards in 1846 was simply one of those ideas whose time had come. And perhaps it was. Or perhaps it was an outstanding example of marketing know-how that many companies and government monopolies would love to replicate today.

❧ The Penny Post ❧

Although Britain had enjoyed a national postal system since its inception in 1635, it was in dire need of reform by the early 1800s because it was complicated, expensive, and different rates applied to different areas of the country. It took years and many people to develop the Uniform Penny Post – the standardisation of British postage rates, with the cheapest stamp costing one penny. The person most widely associated with this reform is Sir Rowland Hill. But another man who was involved in what was considered to be such a highly important innovation was none other than our old friend, Sir Henry Cole. The Treasury awarded him the prize of £100 for his suggestions of how to develop the Penny Post. Whether or not the combination of cards and postage was a deliberate move on his part, the novel idea of sending Christmas cards was certainly made easier by the development of the Penny Post, which was finally introduced on 10 January 1840. It was a massive success.

❧ Christmas stamps ❧

The Post Office began issuing commemorative stamps – special edition stamps issued for a short time to celebrate a particular event – in 1924, to celebrate the British Empire Exhibition. Rather surprisingly, it wasn't until 1 December 1966 that Christmas envelopes first bore festive British stamps.

Two designs were issued – one (which cost three old pence and was designed by Tasveer Shemza) showed King Wenceslas in a glorious gold crown, and the other (costing one shilling and sixpence and designed by James Berry) depicted a snowman wearing a jolly red scarf. Both designers were six years old and were the winners of a stamp design competition held by the children's television programme *Blue Peter*.

Since then, Christmas stamps have featured many different designs, both religious and secular. The Royal Mail now issues Christmas stamps with a religious theme and those with a secular theme in alternate years. For philatelists who still collect first-day covers, the most favoured – and seasonal – postmark comes, fittingly, from the town of Bethlehem. No, not that one. The Bethlehem in question is in Wales.

THE GLASTONBURY THORN

There is nothing unusual about having special decorations that sit on the dining table each Christmas. Most of us have them, and they can be anything from a set of beautiful silver candlesticks to a cotton-wool snowman made by the youngest member of the family. They are part of what makes Christmas special and all are precious, even if for different reasons.

When it comes to the Royal Family's festive decorations, we have no idea of what they like to admire while waiting for the royal sprouts to be dished up. But there is one notable exception. Somewhere among the decorations is a flowering sprig from a hawthorn. It might not look very special but it has tremendous significance for millions of people around the world.

≈ Joseph of Arimathea ≈

The sprig comes from the Glastonbury thorn, a plant in which the story of Jesus and the legend of King Arthur have become intertwined. Legend has it that Joseph of Arimathea, who was a disciple of Jesus Christ (and, some say, his great-uncle), visited Glastonbury after the crucifixion. It is said that Joseph was carrying the Holy Grail, the cup from which Jesus drank at the Last Supper and which was used to catch his blood as he died on the cross. At the time of Joseph's visit, the area around Glastonbury consisted of flooded marshland, so that only high ground was visible. (This land was the famed Isle of Avalon, so essential to the later legend of King Arthur.)

Joseph began to climb the hill that we now know as Wearyall Hill, but he was tired and needed to rest. He thrust his staff (said by some to have once belonged to Jesus himself) into the ground and fell asleep. When he awoke the following morning, the staff had turned into a flowering thorn bush. And so the legend of the Glastonbury thorn was born.

✺ The royal thorn ✺

That first thorn tree has long since perished but it is believed that several of its descendants still grow in Glastonbury, all of them with a provenance that can be traced back to that original thorn. They belong to a particular form of hawthorn (*Crataegus monogyna* 'Biflora') that flowers once in the spring (roughly around Easter) and again at Christmas.

The tradition of cutting a sprig from the Glastonbury thorn and sending it to royalty at Christmas began in the seventeenth century, during the reign of James I, when his consort, Anne of Denmark, was the recipient. The Civil War cast a blight on this practice a few decades later when the Puritans chopped down the original tree, claiming that the beliefs surrounding it were nothing but superstitious nonsense. However, several cuttings from that first precious tree were flourishing unmolested elsewhere in Glastonbury. After the Restoration in 1660, the royal tradition connected with the Glastonbury thorn was eventually revived and has continued ever since.

STIRRING STUFF

In the days before many Christmas foods were easily bought in shops, cooks and housewives took pride in making everything themselves. And one of the centrepieces of the Christmas feast, whether you lived in a mansion or the meanest dwelling, was the plum pudding. Today, it is more commonly known as the Christmas pudding, but its essential ingredients remain the same – dried fruit, suet (whether animal or vegetable), flour or breadcrumbs, eggs, spices and a hefty slosh of alcohol.

Such a rich pudding needs time to mature, so it was always made in advance. However, there was always the danger of forgetting to make it until it was too late. For busy cooks and housewives, their weekly visit to church at the end of November provided a most helpful reminder. The Collect in the Book of Common Prayer for the last Sunday before Advent contains a timely request:

> Stir up, we beseech thee, O Lord, the wills of thy faithful people;
> That they, plenteously bringing forth the fruit of good works,
> may of thee be plenteously rewarded.

Hungry members of the congregation had their own culinary-inspired version of these words. There are several variations, including this one:

> Stir up, we beseech thee, the pudding in the pot,
> Stir up, we beseech thee, and keep it all hot.

Tradition stated that every member of the household must stir the Christmas pudding (preferably from an easterly to a westerly direction, in honour of the Magi who came from the east) and make a wish. Then the mixture was spooned into a pudding basin or a large piece of boiled muslin, securely fastened to prevent water ruining it, and steamed in a large pan on the hob for at least six hours, before being left to cool and carefully stashed away for the great day. The walls of almost every kitchen in Britain must have been running with condensation on Stir-up Sunday, making it Mop-up Sunday too.

BRINGING IN THE YULE LOG

One of the most evocative traditions connected with Christmas is the felling and burning of the Yule log. Not the chocolate variety that is served up to appease those who hate Christmas pudding, but the original massive log that would – all being well – burn merrily from Christmas Eve until Twelfth Night.

The tradition of burning a huge log at the darkest time of the year, to bring warmth and symbolise the return of the sun, is much older than the Christian festival now associated with it. It was originally a pagan ceremony practised by the Norse (the clue is in the name, as 'Yule' is a Norse word), who burned oak logs in honour of their god Thor. When Christianity arrived in England, the Church fathers did their best to put a Christian stamp on this ancient tradition. They ordained that ash was the most appropriate wood for the Yule log, because the baby Jesus was given his first bath in water heated by a fire of ash logs lit by the shepherds who, so the carol says, were 'abiding in the fields'. The shepherds chose ash because it is the only wood to burn well when it's still 'green', or unseasoned. This was presumably based on deductive reasoning, as the Bible does not go into details about the Holy Family's domestic arrangements on the night of Christ's birth.

Any log that is going to burn unceasingly for twelve days will have to be massive, so this was a tradition that could only be enjoyed by those with suitably large fireplaces and rooms. Woe betide the household whose Yule log failed to burn throughout the Twelve Days of Christmas, because bad luck would surely befall them during the coming year. In smaller households, everyone hoped that their more modest Yule log would burn from Christmas Eve until last thing on Christmas night.

To perform the ceremony properly, the tree that would become the Yule log was chosen long in advance and carefully nurtured.

When the time came it was felled, trimmed of branches and often decorated with ribbons. After lashing heavy ropes around it, the adults would drag it to the house where it was going to burn while children danced around and sometimes even rode on the log. (Great fun for them, of course, but it would only have added to the arduous task of dragging the log home.) The log's arrival at the house on Christmas Eve was always greeted with a celebratory drink. Whoever lit the log had to wash their hands well first, otherwise superstition dictated that the log wouldn't burn properly.

Although all members of the household were welcome around the burning log, some people had to keep away, regardless of their status in the house. Anyone with a squint wasn't allowed anywhere near the log, for fear of them bringing bad luck. The same was true for any woman with bare or flat feet. Despite these strictures, it was believed that the Yule log burnt away the year's arguments and resentments, fostering good will and harmony.

On Twelfth Night, when all the decorations were removed from the house, the Yule log was extinguished. Whatever remained was carefully stored ready for the next Christmas Eve, when it would be used to light the new Yule log. The Yule log's ashes were put to good use, too, because they were deemed to have magical properties. If dug into the vegetable patch they would add fertility to the soil, with the bonus of also protecting the house from fire and lightning.

FRIENDLY FIRE

Man has connected fire with the midwinter solstice for millennia. At the darkest time of the year it was not only symbolic to lighten the darkness with warming fires, reminding people that the sun would return and the days would slowly lengthen, but also a comforting necessity.

As a result of what was once our complete dependence on fire for cooking, heating and protection from wild animals, we have developed a variety of midwinter traditions connected with fire.

∽ Bless this ship ∽

Fishermen need all the luck they can get because of the perils of putting out to sea. It was a popular custom for the owner of a boat to bless her, either at Christmas or on New Year's Day, by carrying a flaming brand around her while she was safely berthed in the harbour. This, it was believed, would keep witches away from her for the following year.

∽ Candles ∽

In households that had the money (because decent candles were expensive items), it was traditional to buy a massive candle that would burn throughout Christmas Day. The head of the family would light what was often known as the Yule candle first thing on Christmas morning. It was deemed to be hideously bad luck if the candle burnt out before midnight. In Victorian times especially, these Yule candles were often given by grocers to their most favoured customers in the run-up to Christmas.

❧ Got a light? ❧

It was once considered very bad news to let any sort of fire go out on Christmas Day, especially in the days before the invention of matches. You ran the risk of inviting ill fortune to be your companion for the coming year. If by some mishap every fire in your home was extinguished, you most certainly could not beg a light from your neighbour for the rest of the day. In some areas, this rule extended to the entire Twelve Days of Christmas, whereas in others it only applied on Christmas Day or New Year's Day. It was believed that if anything left the house on those days, even a tiny flame, the result would be the most appalling bad luck. To counter the hardship that the lack of a fire would cause, many villages kept a communal bonfire burning throughout the Christmas period.

❧ Lots of logs ❧

Any unmarried woman who was eager to know when she was going to walk down the aisle was advised to venture out after dark on Christmas night and head for the woodpile. She would gather up an armful of logs without counting them and bring them indoors. There the logs had to stay, completely untouched, until the following morning, when the woman would nervously count them. If she had brought in an even number of logs, she could expect to be married during the following twelve months. An uneven number of logs, on the other hand, meant she wouldn't be disturbing her bottom drawer for at least another year.

❧ Making an ash of it ❧

Only an unbeliever would throw out the ashes from their fires on Christmas Day. Doing so apparently meant that you were throwing the ashes straight into the face of Christ.

❧ Shadows on the wall ❧

Even the shadows cast by the fire carried an element of luck. All was well if someone's shadow was intact, but it was a terrible portent of doom if their shadow appeared without its head because superstition decreed that they would be dead within the year.

❧ The ashen faggot ❧

Burning the ashen faggot was once a very popular Christmas custom in the West Country and especially Devon. Not only was it a source of merriment and good cheer, it was also considered to keep the Devil and all his works at bay. A bundle of ash sticks and twigs, known as a faggot, would be bound with several withies (flexible stalks) of green ash. Ideally, these were cut from the same tree from which the faggot came.

The faggot was carried home and lit using a fragment of the previous year's ashen faggot, and everyone would gather round the fire to watch. Every time a withy burst, it was customary to toast it with a drink. Clearly, this was an excellent incentive to bind the faggot with as many withies as possible.

Unmarried girls who wanted to know when they would be married would each choose a withy and watch it with a beady eye. The owner of the first withy that burst in the fire would be the first girl to marry.

HURRY UP, CHRISTMAS!

You know how it is. Christmas never comes quickly enough when we're children. The days seem to drag themselves out interminably, and December begins to feel like the entire year bolted together. The reverse happens for most of us when we're adults, with the December days rushing past us at headlong speed, especially when our Christmas preparations are on a frustrating go-slow.

One classic way for children to count off the days between 1 December and Christmas Eve is with some form of Advent calendar. Today, these come in all sorts of shapes and sizes, including elaborate fabric hangings with twenty-four pockets, each of which holds a small gift. Traditionalist parents might opt for a cardboard Advent calendar with twenty-four little windows, each of which opens to reveal a Christmassy image (which can be sacred or secular). Parents hoping to bribe their little darlings into coming down to breakfast in good time might choose a chocolate-filled Advent calendar. Adults without children often go for the chocolate option too. Well, it is Christmas.

As with several other Christmas customs now so firmly embedded in our national psyche that we rarely think to question them, Advent calendars originated in Germany in the nineteenth century. Whoever came up with the idea hit on a winner. It is thought that the first handmade Advent calendar was created in 1851, while the first printed example appeared between 1900 and 1910. Some authorities state that the first printed Advent calendar was manufactured in 1902 in Hamburg, while others claim it was in Swabia in 1908. Regardless of when it was first sold, the idea quickly caught on and spread around the world.

And then came the Second World War. Paper shortages, strict rationing of essential commodities and the need for factories to concentrate on manufacturing items that would help the war effort meant that Advent calendars disappeared from sale in all the countries that had once enjoyed them. They didn't reappear until after the war was over.

For parents who had been brought up during the war and had become used to shortages, rationing and the necessity of recycling everything they could, the thought of buying a new Advent calendar for their children each year wasn't always a comfortable one. They had got out of the habit of having new things. One option was to reuse the same calendar year after year, pushing its cardboard windows back into place in the vain hope that they would stay put, and sometimes even having to reapply the glitter that sooner or later always transferred itself to small and eager fingers. However, persuading the children to share a single Advent calendar and expecting them to politely take turns in opening its windows was usually stretching the bounds of frugality to their absolute limits, not to mention inviting tantrums and recriminations even in children doing their best to be good so that Father Christmas would be sure to remember them come Christmas Eve.

HORSEPLAY

Our ancestors certainly knew how to have a good time, and they greeted the imminent arrival of Christmas with all sorts of activities that drew their neighbours into the celebrations. For reasons that are unclear, some of the most notable traditions involved what was quite literally horseplay (plays or entertainments that feature horses). These may have a connection with what was once the equine theme of Boxing Day.

∾ Hoodening ∾

In parts of Kent, it was once traditional for a group of singers, known as hoodeners (pronounced 'oodeners'), to carry around a hobby horse in the run-up to Christmas. (A hobby horse consists of a carved wooden horse's head, decorated with streamers and attached to a long pole. It is mostly associated with traditional May Day celebrations.) The hoodeners went from house to house with their hooden horse, as it was called. Its jaws opened and shut, and the hoodeners would try to ride the horse in comic fashion. Some might even attempt to shoe it, but the hooden horse would respond by shying in a playful and humorous way that, with luck, entertained the occupants of the house while they stood freezing on their doorstep. The hoodeners' antics would be rewarded with food, drink or money, and then they'd be off to the next house. Recently, the tradition of hoodening has been revived in some parts of Kent.

❦ Mari Lwyd ❦

In Wales, the equine tradition involved a horse figure that was often called Mari Lwyd, although it did have a few regional variations, such as being called 'the grey mare' in English-speaking parts of Wales. A horse's skull was fastened to a long pole, kitted out with reins and draped in a white sheet, then carried from house to house by someone with suitably strong arms. The Mari Lwyd figure was accompanied by a group of singers who would visit each house in turn. They abided by a set ritual of singing a few verses of a traditional song that asked for admission into the house. The householder would then continue the ritual by giving lots of reasons, in verse, why the singers couldn't enter their home. This involved plenty of good-humoured joking and ribaldry. If the Mari Lwyd group won the versifying contest, they entered the house and were offered something to eat and drink, and possibly some money too. In return, they might do some more singing, before bidding farewell to the occupants of the house and going on their way.

As with hoodening, the tradition of Mari Lwyd hasn't completely disappeared from Wales, and there is an annual performance at St Fagans National History Museum in Cardiff.

TOLLING THE DEVIL'S KNELL

Before the Protestant Reformation of the sixteenth century, church bells performed a vital function late each Christmas Eve. In each village and town, the church bell was tolled once for every year that had elapsed since Christ's birth. This was fondly known as 'the Old Lad's passing bell', with the 'Old Lad' in question being the Devil.

There are two likely explanations for this. The first is that in an age when countless daily events were superstitiously regarded as portents of evil, this ceremony brought comfort to parishioners because it was deemed to keep the Devil at bay for the coming year. It is similar to the old New Year's Eve custom of opening the windows at midnight and making the loudest racket possible in order to drive out any evil spirits that might be lurking in your home. Although it must have been reassuring to know that the Devil had been vanquished once again on Christmas Eve, the tolling bell had its disadvantages because it would have kept awake anyone who was hoping to have a peaceful nap before turning out for Midnight Mass.

The second explanation is much more theological and is connected to the tradition of tolling 'the passing bell', as it is called, when someone dies: the church bell slowly tolls out the number of years that the person lived. So 'the Old Lad's passing bell' tolled the many hundreds of years since Christ was born and the Devil died.

Although the custom of 'tolling the Devil's knell', as it is now more commonly called, has almost entirely vanished from Britain, it is still kept each Christmas Eve at Dewsbury Minster in West Yorkshire. Black Tom, the tenor bell in the church tower, sonorously tolls from midway through the evening until midnight. The toll begins slightly earlier each Christmas Eve, of course, to account for the extra year, and is carefully timed to finish at exactly the right moment. Rather than being a charm against the Devil, Black Tom's peals are now regarded as a declaration of Christ's victory over evil.

PLEASE GIVE GENEROUSLY

Sometimes the combination of eating and drinking too much and being with one's nearest and dearest for days on end can be a little trying. Which, you might imagine, is why Christmas Day is followed by the day known as Boxing Day. Perhaps this is the day when tempers, frayed beyond endurance by close proximity to all those relatives that we try to avoid for the rest of the year, finally snap and sparring matches break out over the dinner table.

But no. It seems that Boxing Day got its name for entirely different reasons.

❧ Alms boxes ❧

Centuries before the advent of social security and the imposition of the minimum wage, life could be very tough for many people. They lived a hand-to-mouth existence, so any financial help was always very welcome. Christmas was a good opportunity for this because the wealthier members of a town or village would give alms to the poor. Some sources say that these alms boxes were placed in churches. The congregation would put their contributions into the boxes, which were then opened on 26 December (St Stephen's Day) and their contents divided up and given to the poor of the parish. This was often referred to as 'the dole of the Christmas box'.

∼ A generous tip ∼

Another form of Christmas box involved people in subservient positions asking their superiors for money. They carried earthenware boxes into which the money would be placed. There was a hole for the money to go in but not one for it to come out, so the boxes would be broken open on St Stephen's Day. This custom has continued for centuries in one form or another, and a modified version of it is still in operation today whenever we give a tip or gift to the postman (or postwoman) or the dustmen, even though this is usually handed over before Christmas.

Not everyone is happy with this arrangement and they didn't always like it in the past, either. An edition of *Punch* magazine in 1849 had a good grumble about it:

> The Christmas Box system is, in fact, a piece of horribly internecine strife between cooks and butchers' boys, lamplighters, beadles, and all classes of society, tugging at each other's pockets for the sake of what can be got under the pretext of seasonable benevolence. Our cooks bully our butchers for the annual box, and our butchers take it out on us in the course of the year by tacking false tails on to our saddles of mutton, adding false feet to our legs of lamb, and chousing us with large lumps of chump in our chops, for the purpose of adding to our bills by giving undue weight to our viands. Punch has resolved on the overthrow of the Boxing system, and down it will go before 1849 has expired.

Needless to say, it was unsuccessful.

HUNTING THE WREN

Most Christmas traditions vary from being charming to fairly harmless, but one in particular has less to recommend it. This is the custom, which was practised in Wales, Ireland and the Isle of Man, of hunting a wren on Boxing Day. A team of boys (known as 'wren boys' or 'droluns') or men would catch and kill a couple of wrens, put their bodies in a specially decorated box and parade through the village or town, entertaining everyone they met with songs and dances. These included a special song about the poor wren, which began:

> The wren, the wren, the king of birds
> Was caught on St Stephen's Day in the furze.

Sometimes the wren was hung on a branch of holly and then given a funeral later.

You might wonder what the wren had done to warrant such unfortunate attention. One theory is that it is revenge, after a wren once acted as a snitch at a crucial moment in a war when a group of British soldiers was about to ambush the enemy. Instead of keeping quiet, as any patriotic bird should surely do, it pecked at a drum and thereby alerted the enemy to the presence of the waiting Britons. Which war and which enemy? Take your pick, because they vary according to who is telling the story.

People on the Isle of Man tell a different tale. According to them, many sailors were lured to their death by the beautiful singing of a siren. She was about to be caught but managed to escape at the last minute by turning into a wren and flying away. So each Christmas, after the wren hunt, the feathers of the dead birds were used by sailors as charms to protect them from shipwrecks.

You might also wonder how it is that the wren, which is such a tiny creature, can possibly be the king of the bird kingdom, as described in the wren boys' traditional song. According to an old folktale, there was once a competition among the birds to see which of them deserved to be called the king. It looked as though the eagle was going to win, as it soared higher and higher in the sky. But just as it reached the point where it couldn't climb any further, a tiny wren slipped out from its hiding place within the eagle's feathers and flew a few inches higher, thereby tricking the eagle and earning the title of 'king'.

VOICES OUT OF THE AIR

Many people have a long list of Christmas essentials without which 25 December simply wouldn't be the same. And one of these is watching, or listening to, the Christmas royal broadcast.

In the 1930s, the wireless, or 'listening in' as it was sometimes called, was still a fairly novel invention: BBC radio broadcasts had only begun in 1922. Ten years after those initial broadcasts, in 1932, John Reith, who was the first managing director of the BBC, came up with what was then a rather daring idea. He suggested that King George V should broadcast a Christmas message to the Empire, to launch the new Empire Service (which later became the World Service). George V wasn't too keen on the notion at first, but felt much happier about the proposal after visiting the BBC's offices that summer.

On Christmas Day 1932, the king duly read out a message to the Empire. The time chosen was 3pm, although the broadcast actually began five minutes late. It was short (it only lasted two and a half minutes) and to the point, and the words had been written by Rudyard Kipling. George V began by saying, 'I speak now from my home and my heart to you all; to men and women so cut off by the snows, the desert, or the sea, that only voices out of the air can reach them.' His voice 'out of the air' reached 20 million listeners, and the experiment was such a success that George V continued to broadcast on Christmas Day until 1935, shortly before his death in January 1936. Even so, a Christmas royal message wasn't yet an annual tradition.

King George VI, who famously battled with a life-long stammer, delivered his first Christmas message in 1937. There was no message in 1938, but it was imperative to give one in 1939, as war with Germany had broken out on 3 September that year. Queen Elizabeth had recently read 'God Knows', a poem by Minnie Louise Haskins, and suggested to her husband that he should include its opening lines in his 1939 Christmas broadcast. It was the perfect choice for a nation facing an uncertain and frightening future:

And I said to the man who stood at the gate of the year: 'Give
    me a light that I may tread safely into the unknown.'
And he replied: 'Go out into the darkness and put your hand
    into the Hand of God.
That shall be to you better than light and safer than a known way.'

The Christmas broadcast became an annual event (with one exception) from 1951, which was also the year of George VI's final broadcast. He was too ill to read it live, so it was recorded in advance. He died on 6 February 1952.

In 1957, the Christmas broadcast given by Queen Elizabeth II, his daughter and successor to the throne, was televised for the first time. As with her previous radio broadcasts, it was transmitted live.

The one exception in the otherwise unbroken line of broadcasts since 1951 came in 1969, when the Queen issued a written message instead. The groundbreaking television documentary, *Royal Family*, had been broadcast that summer and the Queen had felt that this was probably quite enough televised royalty for one year.

All the palaver of recording the broadcast live on Christmas Day must surely have cast a slight pall over the royal festive lunch. It is difficult to imagine stuffing down an extra roast potato or another mince pie with reckless abandon when you know you've got to address the nation and the Commonwealth in a few minutes. So the Queen must have been very relieved from 1960 onwards when the broadcasts came to be pre-recorded, to allow time for the recordings to be sent round the world. From now on, she was able to enjoy the royal Christmas lunch without the prospect of having to face the television cameras immediately afterwards.

The royal Christmas message was the sole preserve of the BBC until 1997, when a new regime was introduced. The broadcasts now alternate every two years between ITV and the BBC. This was radical enough, but 1997 was also the first year when the Christmas broadcast appeared on the Internet.

The traditional broadcast might have embraced the latest technology, but its central tenet – of the sovereign addressing his or her people – remained unchanged.

A VERY SPECIAL GIFT

Each November, a massive fir tree is felled with great ceremony in one of the forests outside Oslo in Norway. Of course, thousands of its fellow trees meet the same fate at this time of year but this tree, which is usually a Norwegian spruce (*Picea abies*), is different. It will have been specially chosen, because only the best tree will do: the tree in question is always referred to as 'the queen of the forest'. The ceremonial severing of the tree's trunk from its roots (it is lifted into the air by a huge crane rather than allowed to fall sideways) will be witnessed by several dignitaries, including the British Ambassador to Norway, the Lord Mayor of Westminster and the Mayor of Oslo. That is because this is the tree that will cross the North Sea by boat and then be taken by road to Trafalgar Square in London, where it will be erected with the help of hydraulic lifts and dressed with vertical strings of hundreds of white lights.

The Trafalgar Square Christmas tree is one of the most celebrated features of Christmas in London, and it has been the December centrepiece of this most British of squares since 1947. The plaque that always stands at the bottom of the tree says it all:

> This tree is given by the city of Oslo as a token of Norwegian gratitude to the people of London for their assistance during the years 1940–45. A tree has been given annually since 1947.

This refers to the years during the Second World War when Norway was under German control. King Haakon VII, his family and government were evacuated by the British Navy and made it safely to London, where the king set up a government-in-exile for the rest of the war.

The tree's lights are switched on in a special ceremony, led by the Lord Mayor of Westminster, on the first Thursday in December. It is still there during what are often quite riotous New Year's Eve celebrations in Trafalgar Square, but is dismantled and taken away shortly before Twelfth Night. In common with many other discarded Christmas trees, it is turned into bark chippings and used as a mulch for plants.

In the meantime, in a forest somewhere near Oslo, another tree is being lovingly prepared for the honour of symbolising over seventy years of friendship between two European countries.

Seeing in the New Year

Ring out the old, ring in the new,
Ring, happy bells, across the snow:
The year is going, let him go;
Ring out the false, ring in the true.

'In Memoriam', Alfred, Lord Tennyson

THE OLD NEW YEAR

We take so many facets of our daily lives for granted that often we never even stop to consider when they began. Take the New Year festivities, for instance. You might imagine that they have always taken place on the final day of December and the first day of January. But the story isn't quite that simple.

❧ Ancient cultures ❧

Four thousand years ago, different cultures celebrated their new year at various times of the solar year. In about 2000 BC, the new year for the Ancient Babylonians began at the first New Moon following the spring equinox (on or near 21 March). Some other cultures, including the Egyptians, favoured the New Moon following the autumn equinox (on or near 23 September).

❧ The Roman calendar ❧

Our annual calendar of twelve months was devised by the Romans, but it didn't begin in January in the way it does now. Instead, the year began on 1 March, and the names for the months from September to December referred to their numerical position within the year: September was the seventh month, October the eighth, November the ninth and December the tenth. All this changed in 153 BC, when it was officially announced that the New Year would now begin on 1 January (the month named for Janus, the two-faced god who simultaneously looked towards the future and back to the past). The festival to celebrate the New Year was called Kalendae.

New Year gifts

The Romans enjoyed plenty of feasting and frolicking during Saturnalia, the midwinter festival dedicated to their god Saturn which ran, at its peak, from 17–23 December. They now had three more days of celebration at Kalendae, which was devoted to the Sabine goddess Strenia. During Kalendae, Romans exchanged small gifts known as *strenae*, which frequently consisted of foods such as honey and pastries. They gave one another coins, too, which often bore an image of Janus on one side and a ship on the other. They also decked their homes with sprays of greenery, including laurel leaves, because the laurel bush was associated with the goddess Strenia.

The arrival of Christianity

Both Saturnalia and Kalendae disappeared when the Roman Empire converted to Christianity in the fourth century, but for centuries afterwards people continued the custom of exchanging gifts at the turn of the year in January. This was true in Britain, too, whether the gifts were lavish or frugal, and this state of affairs continued until the mid-nineteenth century when Christmas gradually became the customary time for gift-giving.

When Christianity first became established in Europe, many Christians preferred to spend the New Year period in contemplation and fasting, rather than copying the Romans in having a rollicking good time. However, this self-restraint gradually gave way until the

New Year was once again a good opportunity to have as much fun as possible.

❧ Changing the date ❧

Despite Julius Caesar confirming in 45 AD that the New Year began on 1 January, it didn't stay that way in Britain. Although in post-Roman times Britons continued to celebrate the beginning of January with New Year festivities, legally each year now began on 25 March. And that state of affairs continued until 1600 in Scotland, and until 1752 in England, Wales, Ireland and the British Empire when, once again, the legal New Year officially switched back to 1 January.

Happy New Year!

PREPARING FOR THE NEW YEAR

For centuries, people have believed that the start of the New Year must be as auspicious as possible because this will ensure happiness and prosperity during the rest of the year. Equally, a strained or disastrous New Year's Day is thought to presage a difficult year. This has led to many traditions about how to begin the New Year, some of which are better known than others.

❧ Spick and span ❧

If you want to ensure a good year ahead, it's essential for your home to be spotless come New Year's Eve. Everything must be clean and tidy, in readiness for the New Year. In Scotland, this special cleaning session was known as 'redding'. The fireplace had to be swept out, and the ashes were examined closely because the patterns and shapes they made were believed to foretell the future.

The state of your personal finances must also be pristine by the time midnight arrives. You are supposed to clear your debts, so you can begin the New Year with a clean financial slate. This might be a laudable aim but it is difficult to see how some of us can manage it so soon after forking out a modest fortune for Christmas gifts, food and all the other festive necessities.

❧ Out with the old and in with the new ❧

Everything really livens up as soon as midnight arrives on New Year's Eve. Tradition dictates that you must let out the old year before welcoming in the new one. This might simply mean opening the back door, so the old year can exit, before opening the front door so the new year can enter. Alternatively, if you feel the need, it might mean flinging open every door and window at midnight and making the most appalling racket, so the old year flies out (accompanied by any mischievous or evil spirits that might be hiding in corners) before the new year rushes in. Whether you feel capable of doing this could well be connected to how devotedly you've been celebrating the demise of one year and the start of the next. For some of us, hearing the clattering of saucepan lids at midnight could be close to torture.

❧ Pucker up ❧

Even if you aren't interested in any of the other customs associated with New Year's Eve, this one might appeal. No sooner has midnight arrived than the kissing begins. Sometimes, everyone kisses everyone else. And sometimes they only kiss their nearest neighbours, in which case some clever strategy might come in handy if you want to make sure you're standing close to those you want to kiss and far away from the ones you would rather avoid.

✎ For the sake of auld lang syne ✎

We may have forgotten many of the traditions our forebears performed religiously every year, but one eighteenth-century custom that originated in Scotland remains when midnight strikes on 31 December. Everyone shuffles into a circle, crosses their arms and grabs the hand of the person next to them, and begins singing (or mumbling) the chorus of 'Auld Lang Syne'. If they can manage the verses as well, they probably haven't had enough to drink.

It is often claimed that the words of 'Auld Lang Syne' were written by Robert Burns, one of Scotland's foremost poets, but this is not entirely true. In fact he heard some of the words when an old man recited them to him, after which Burns copied them down and, in 1788, wrote the rest of the poem himself. Burns was an avid collector of old Scots songs, and always made it plain that 'Auld Lang Syne' was based on one of these.

✎ First footing ✎

Although this tradition has declined somewhat in recent years it is still an essential part of New Year for many people. It is often thought to belong exclusively to Scotland, but it was practised more widely than that, especially in the nineteenth and twentieth centuries.

'First footing' refers to the first person who steps over a house's threshold after midnight on New Year's Eve. It is essential for this person to confer luck on the house, so they must abide by a list of strict criteria. Usually, the first footer must be a dark-haired man – despite the rise of feminism, it has long been deemed extremely unlucky for it to be a woman. This man must not have red hair, flat feet or a squint (three characteristics that are also considered very bad news on board ship, strangely enough), and ideally he should be a stranger. Tradition also dictates that he must be carrying items that will bring prosperity to the household, such as money, a lump of coal or some food. Of course, it is highly unlikely that such a man will be aimlessly wandering the streets, loaded down with bags full of propitious objects, just waiting to hop over the threshold the moment midnight strikes. He is far more likely to be the friend of a friend at a New Year's Eve party, who can be persuaded to put down his drink, step outside while clutching the remains of the garlic bread and come back in to the amusement of the assembled company.

❦ Money in your pocket ❦

After the New Year's Eve celebrations are over and you've tottered off to bed, you might imagine that your traditional duties have finished. But they haven't. If you want to make sure that the coming year will be a prosperous one, you must begin New Year's Day with money in your pocket, even if you aren't going to spend it. It is also advisable to be looking your best, with your hair clean and brushed, and in decent clothes.

❦ Feeding the cattle ❦

People who relied on farming for their livelihood always made sure they didn't forget their animals during the New Year celebrations. In the north of England it was once traditional to feed your Christmas bunch of mistletoe to the first cow that calved after New Year's Day, to guard against witchcraft. This is because witches were notorious for turning milk sour – something that would be a complete disaster for anyone whose supply of milk, butter and cheese depended on the health of their own herd of cattle.

❦ Water traditions ❦

Water also played an important part in the traditional New Year celebrations. In the days when the only way for people to get fresh water was to draw it from the nearest well, the first drawing of water after midnight chimed was believed to be extra special. It was called the 'cream of the well', and was thought to confer beauty and good fortune on any woman who was lucky enough to wash in it.

In some parts of South Wales, young men walked around their villages with buckets of fresh water drawn from the local spring. They would call at each house and sprinkle each person they met with some of the water (whether they were up and dressed or still languishing in bed), in exchange for a little money. It is easy to imagine some people with serious hangovers – or who didn't want to be caught in bed because of who was there with them – paying these young men to keep away. Some New Year traditions, even when practised with the best of intentions, might turn out to be not so lucky after all.

HAPPY HOGMANAY!

Hogmanay and Scotland go together like bread and butter or, to use a Scottish analogy, neeps and tatties. In Scotland, Christmas isn't nearly as important a celebration as New Year's Eve, or Hogmanay. That's when the fun and games really start.

❧ The roots of the past ❧

In the sixteenth century, the Protestant Reformation gained a strong hold in Scotland. One of its first casualties was Christmas, which was effectively struck off the calendar completely because it wasn't mentioned in the Bible and therefore should not be celebrated. The same was true, of course, for the New Year. This most certainly wasn't mentioned in the Bible, being a secular celebration, and it was heavily frowned upon because of the opportunity it presented for people to let down their hair and misbehave.

But midwinter in Scotland is a time when the days are very short and the nights very long, and when people need something to cheer them up. Christmas and Hogmanay gradually re-emerged, but Christmas had become very much the lesser of the two festivals. Hogmanay was now the main event in the midwinter celebrations.

It's uncertain how Hogmanay (and its variant spellings, such as 'Hagmenay') got its name. There are several theories about its etymology, including the idea that it comes from the Old French, *aguillanneuf*, which was the word for both the New Year and a gift given at the New Year. Regardless of its derivation, this dual meaning of Hogmanay was still common in the late eighteenth century. In 1790, an issue of *The Gentleman's Magazine* stated, 'In Scotland, and in the North of England, till very lately, it was customary for every body to make and receive presents amongst their friends on the eve of the new year, which present was called an Hagmenay.'

Christmas has accumulated a collection of begging customs and the same is true of Hogmanay. Even in the early twentieth century, children would gather in front of their neighbours' houses and chant rhymes or sing songs in the hope of being rewarded with a small cake or something to drink. Whether this was to congratulate them on their melodious voices or make them go away is a moot point.

❧ Hogmanay fire ceremonies ❧

As well as Hogmanay being an excuse to be lit up with alcohol, it has also long been a focus for celebratory fire ceremonies. These must surely have a strong connection with the return of the sun's light at the winter solstice. Although many of these traditional ceremonies have now disappeared, a few are still a feature in some parts of Scotland. In Stonehaven, near Aberdeen, for instance, there is an annual Fireballs Ceremony, in which people wrap flammable material, such as paper, in balls made from chicken wire, set light to them at midnight and parade up and down the streets while swinging the balls around their heads. Any balls that are still burning when the ceremony ends are flung into the harbour.

Another Hogmanay custom, called Burning the Clavie, is still celebrated at Burghead on the Moray Firth, but it takes place on 11 January, which is Old New Year's Day (using the Julian calendar). The clavie in question is half a barrel, which is fixed to a pole, filled with tar, ignited with a brand (but never with matches) and paraded around the town in a procession led by the Clavie King. It is then carried to the top of nearby Doorie Hill and placed on a ruined Roman altar. When the burning clavie collapses, everyone grabs a piece and takes it home so they can light their own fires with it. The charcoal remains of these pieces of the clavie are traditionally stuffed up the chimney to keep witches and evil spirits at bay during the coming year.

CALENNIG

In Wales and its adjoining English counties, New Year's Day has long been marked by a tradition in which adults go from house to house, wishing the occupants a happy new year and collecting something in return for their trouble. This 'something' was once known as a *calennig*, or New Year's gift, and was usually food or money.

As time went by, the adults hovered in the background, or stayed at home, and it was children who did the rounds. By now, they carried a *calennig* themselves, and it conveyed a blessing on everyone who saw it. It was traditionally an apple skewered with three sticks to make a tripod, studded with nuts or cloves, and decorated with a sprig of thyme, rosemary or some other evergreen herb. The children would sing a song that spelled out their requirements, so no householder was left in any doubt about what they were expecting. This song was popular in Cardiganshire and Pembrokeshire:

> Mi godais heddiw ma's o'm tŷ
> A'm cwd a'm pastwn gyda mi,
> A dyma'm neges ar eich traws,
> Sef llanw'm cwd â bara a chaws.

It translates as:

> I left my house today
> With my bag and my stick,
> And here is my message to you.
> Fill my bag with bread and cheese.

The *calennig* tradition still continues in some parts of Wales and nearby English counties, but today the children are most likely to receive some shiny new pennies.

NEW YEAR RESOLUTIONS

We've been making New Year resolutions for millennia. It seems there is something intrinsically human about hoping that the coming year will be more prosperous and happy than the one that's passing, and that we'll become a better version of ourselves.

⇌ The history of New Year resolutions ⇌

At the turn of each year, the Ancient Babylonians would promise their gods that they'd honour their debts and return any objects they'd borrowed. The Romans also made morally based resolutions at the start of each year.

The idea of making New Year resolutions particularly appealed to Puritans who became prevalent in the sixteenth and seventeenth centuries, with the rise of the Protestant Reformation. Even though the Puritans were effectively given the thumbs-down by many people from the 1660s onwards, their desire to make resolutions each January remained.

⇌ Doomed to failure? ⇌

We may jot down our New Year resolutions at the start of January with the best of intentions, but many of us have often broken them – or possibly even forgotten them – by the time February arrives.

Take Samuel Pepys, a man who always liked to enjoy himself. On 31 December 1661, he wrote in his diary, 'I have newly taken a solemn oath about abstaining from plays and wine, which I am resolved to keep.' As with so many New Year resolutions, temptation was not far away and proved irresistible. Less than three weeks later, on 20 January 1662, Pepys took delivery of 'four gallons of Malaga wine; what it will stand us in I know not; but it is the first great quantity of wine that I ever bought.'

Mark Twain, the nineteenth-century American writer, was under no illusions about the benefits of making New Year resolutions. 'New Year's Day ... now is the accepted time to make your regular annual good resolutions. Next week you can begin paving hell with them as usual.' Oscar Wilde, who was Twain's contemporary, had an equally sardonic view. 'Good resolutions are simply cheques that men draw on a bank where they have no account.'

A Gladsome Noise

Wassail and wassail, all over the town!
The cup it is white and the ale it is brown.

'Somerset Wassail', traditional carol

HERE WE COME A-WASSAILING

English is a fascinating melting pot of languages acquired from other countries, especially those whose kings once occupied our throne. So it's hardly surprising that the word 'wassail' is thought to have come from the Old Norse *ves heill*, which means to be in good health. The Old English version of this was *wes hal*, from which we get the word 'hale' (meaning 'healthy'). And, of course, it also gives us 'wassail'.

In the eleventh and twelfth centuries, if you wanted to toast someone's health you would say 'wassail', to which the accepted response was 'drinkhail'. Over the following centuries, the meaning of 'wassail' expanded from being a simple drinking toast to the cheerful practice of visiting your neighbours at Christmas and offering them a drink from the wassail bowl you were carrying while you sang them a song. Although both sexes could do this, it was much more customary for women to do the rounds. The contents of the bowl varied, but the traditional wassail drink was mulled ale mixed with spices and topped with pulped roasted apples, and which was often known as lamb's wool because that's exactly what it looked like.

Sometimes the words of the wassail song spelled out precisely what its listeners were expected to do, so there was no danger of misunderstanding. This rhyme comes from Worcestershire, which is a prime apple-growing county:

> Wassail, wassail, through the town,
> If you've got any apples throw them down,
> Up with the stocking and down with the shoe,
> If you've got no apples, money will do.

☙ Bang bang! ❧

By the seventeenth century, these wassailing parties were performing an additional service for apple farmers, especially in the southern and south-western parts of England. There was no set date for this sort of wassailing, although it always took place at some point during the Christmas season. After offering the occupants of the house a drink from the wassail bowl and serenading them, the wassailers would go into the orchards and bless the trees. They did this in a variety of ways, from drinking a glass of cider in honour of the trees, to placing food (often bread soaked in cider) around a tree's roots or in its branches, to unleashing a volley of gunfire (which may have been intended to frighten away any evil spirits lurking in the orchard).

Wassailing in orchards has been revived in some parts of Britain in recent years, while in others it has never really gone away.

WAITY MATTERS

Long before Britain had an official police force, many medieval towns were patrolled at night by paid watchmen who announced the passing hours and carried horns or trumpets, so they could alert the sleeping populace if necessary. By the middle of the fifteenth

century, some of these waits, as they were known, were so celebrated that they were invited to go abroad on important national
expeditions, such as that of Edward IV to France in 1475. They also
played music at civic functions in their home towns, and some were
given liveries to wear while doing so. They patrolled some towns and
cities throughout the year, but in other places they were only on
duty between November and February.

By the middle of the sixteenth century, waits were employed less
for their muscle power and more for their musicianship. Not that
everyone agreed about their musical talents. Ned Ward, in his 1703
book *The London Spy*, described one discordant encounter with a
group of waits.

> We heard a noise so dreadful and surprising that we thought
> the devil was riding on hunting thro' the city, with a pack of
> deep-mouth'd hellhounds... I ask'd my friend what was the
> meaning of this infernal outcry?... 'Why, these are the city waits,
> who play every winter's night thro' the streets to rouse each lazy
> drone to family duty!'

Changes to the way municipal boroughs operated meant that many
waits vanished after the 1840s. But not all, by any means. And it
seems that those who remained were often as noisy and ear-piercing
as the band of men that Ned Ward wrote about.

In the Victorian era, December issues of *Punch* magazine were often filled with complaints about the nuisance value of Christmas waits who woke people up at night with their music (or noise, depending on their level of musical talent). In his book *Second Thoughts of an Idle Fellow*, published in 1898, Jerome K Jerome described throwing coal out of his window at some Christmas waits. After vainly chucking about twenty lumps of coal at them, he finally scored a hit, only to discover that his unwitting target was a neighbour who'd gone into the street to ask the waits to shut up.

But not everyone disliked Christmas waits. Washington Irving, in *The Sketch Book of Geoffrey Crayon, Gent.*, first published in 1819, thought differently. Writing as the pseudonymous Geoffrey Crayon, he described his experience of hearing them one winter's night:

> I had scarcely got into bed when a strain of music seemed to break forth in the air just below the window. I listened, and found it proceeded from a band, which I concluded to be the waits from some neighbouring village. They went round the house, playing under the windows. I drew aside the curtains to hear them more distinctly. The moon-beams fell through the upper part of the casement, partially lighting up the antiquated apartment. The sounds, as they receded, became more soft and aerial, and seemed to accord with quiet and moon-light. I listened and listened – they became more and more tender and remote, and as they gradually died away my head sank upon the pillow, and I fell asleep.

Sweet singing in the choir

They can be moving and slow, they can be merry and vigorous. They can be old or contemporary, beautiful or banal, but would Christmas be the same without a few carols?

≈ The oldest carols ≈

Although it might seem impossible to believe this next time you are listening to a solemn, possibly even mawkish, Victorian carol, in medieval times it was customary to dance in a circle while singing carols. Only traces are left of these early carols but it seems they were jolly, lively and communal tunes. They were sung at a variety of gatherings, but not in church because they were a form of folk music. Most began and ended with a refrain, or burden (in other words, a repeating phrase), and were interspersed with verses, or stanzas. Some of these carols were country dances, enjoyed by ordinary people. Others were danced at the English court, where French fashions, etiquette and language held so much sway. These courtly dances were direct descendants of the French *caroles*, which were social dances that first became popular in France in the twelfth century. Sadly, very little is known about them today.

Another form of carol was the festival song – something that was only sung at a particular time of year. One example of this is 'The Boar's Head Carol', in its various versions, which is only sung on or near 16 December.

Some carols contained amorous symbolism and were part of the elaborate courtly games that were particularly popular in the sixteenth century. The lyrics of these carols sometimes contained hidden meanings. For instance, the carol 'The Holly and the Ivy' that we still sing today has coded references to the relationship between men (represented by holly) and women (represented by ivy).

And, of course, many carols contained straightforward religious themes, even though they may still have originally been sung as the accompaniment to dances. Although we now associate carols exclusively with Christmas, that was not always the case. For instance, there are a few carols for the Annunciation (such as the fifteenth-century 'Hayl, Mary, ful of grace') and for Candlemas (such as 'Letabundas'). But no matter what the occasion, all carols would be sung or danced in a circle, with the structure of refrain and verse.

❦ Loss and revival ❦

These medieval carols, whether intended for Christmas or some other time of year, were beautiful and often featured intricate cross rhythms. Sadly, they were not to last. The Protestant Reformation in the sixteenth and seventeenth centuries almost completely wiped them out and they were replaced by sung psalms. The gradual rise of Puritanism meant that religious festivals were first frowned upon and then actively discouraged, if not completely banned. Although people in rural areas, far away from the prying eyes of Parliamentarian soldiers, might have continued to celebrate Christmas with the help of medieval carols, anyone who lived in a town had little chance of getting away with such outright civil disobedience.

Popular carols continued after the Restoration in 1660, but the courtly carols had all but vanished. New carols were written and published each Christmas, often on broadsheets decorated with woodcuts. In the nineteenth century there was a gradual interest in reviving older carols, which formed an interesting contrast to the new carols that were being written, such as 'O Come, O Come, Emmanuel' and 'O Little Town of Bethlehem'. Today, many of us feel that a carol service wouldn't be complete without a good mixture of ancient and more modern carols.

O COME, LET US SING

For many of us, music is an essential feature of Christmas. We can soon get fed up with the seemingly endless round of festive pop songs that boom out from every shop from early October onwards, but religious music still has the power to send a shiver down the spine, and especially so if we can enjoy it in the company of other people in a carol concert or special church service.

◈ Midnight Mass ◈

Christians have been attending Midnight Mass for centuries. The service begins either shortly before midnight on Christmas Eve or at midnight itself, because it was once believed that Christ was born at midnight. It consists of a formal service of prayers and carols, with Holy Communion for those who are allowed to participate.

Midnight Mass was first celebrated in the basilica of St Mary Major in Rome in the fifth century, but it could only be celebrated by the Pope until the twelfth century, when priests were allowed to conduct Midnight Mass too. In those days, of course, the Christian religion was exclusively Roman Catholic.

◈ The Festival of Nine Lessons and Carols ◈

You don't have to be a practising Christian, or even a believer at all, to find the Festival of Nine Lessons and Carols very powerful. It follows a set pattern, with nine Bible readings that describe the fall of man, the angels telling of the coming of Jesus and the story of his birth, interspersed with prayers and nine carols.

The first service was conducted in 1880 by EW Benson, the first Bishop of Truro (he became Archbishop of Canterbury in 1883), and GHS Walpole (later the Bishop of Edinburgh). It took place at 10pm on Christmas Eve in the wooden building that acted as Truro Cathedral while the real cathedral was being built. The service was a big success and was soon adopted by other churches and cathedrals.

Today, listeners from across the world are able to hear and watch the service live from the chapel at King's College, Cambridge. It was first held here in 1918 and first broadcast by the BBC in 1928 and has continued, more or less unchanged, ever since. (The only year that the BBC missed was 1930.) The service even continued throughout the Second World War, despite all the old and precious glass having been removed for safety from the windows of the chapel, making it very draughty for those inside.

The service always begins with the processional carol, 'Once in Royal David's City', sung by a solo chorister. The chorister in question is only chosen shortly before the service begins, to avoid him being paralysed by pre-performance nerves.

≈ Oiel Verrey ≈

This is a tradition from the Isle of Man. Its name is a corruption of *Oie feaill Voirrey*, which means 'Eve of Mary's feast'. After the candlelit service ended on Christmas Eve, members of the congregation would stay in church and anyone who felt like it would get to their feet and sing a *carval* (the Manx word for carol). This was quite a rowdy event, by all accounts, as the women of the congregation would throw things, such as dried peas, at their boyfriends or husbands when they stood up to sing. When Oiel Verrey ended, everyone would go off in search of some hot ale, and the celebrations would continue until it was time to fall into bed or pass out, whichever came first.

❦ *Plygain* ❦

Welsh voices and music are a perfect combination, and for centuries they were a special feature of Christmas morning in towns and villages throughout Wales when everyone came together to enjoy the *plygain* (which, when translated into English, means 'cockcrow') service at their local church. The service, which originated in pre-Reformation Wales but somehow survived the changes that Protestantism brought, took place before dawn, at some point between 3am and 6am, and people would while away the hours before the service in a variety of ways, including torchlight processions, dances and toffee-making.

The service, which consisted of prayers and carols, was always held by candlelight, not only for its beauty and religious symbolism (representing Jesus as the Light of the World), but out of necessity because Welsh church services were usually held in daylight so there was no provision for night-time illumination. Each member of the congregation brought a candle, and the result was frequently quite magical. One strict rule was that no carol could be sung more than once, even if it had a different musical arrangement. After the prayers were over, the unaccompanied carol singing often continued until dawn broke, by which time hunger sent the congregation home in search of breakfast.

Plygain is enjoying a revival in some parts of Wales, although the service is now held at a later time on Christmas Day or on some other day between then and Epiphany. Traditionally, women were excluded from singing carols during the service, although this is now starting to change in some churches and chapels.

WHO WAS GOOD KING WENCESLAS?

We sing about him every Christmas in the eponymous carol, which tells us that the 'good king' and his page ventured out in the snow on the feast of Stephen (26 December) to take food, wine and logs to a man who was struggling to collect firewood. But most of us haven't a clue whether this is simply a story or if there really was a Good King Wenceslas.

❧ Family problems ❧

The carol does concern a real person – Wenceslas, Duke of Bohemia, who lived in the tenth century. Fortunately, bearing in mind its seasonal nature, the carol fails to mention the most memorable fact about the real Wenceslas, which is that he was assassinated in his native Bohemia in 935. He was murdered in a plot that is thought to have been hatched by his brother, the aptly named Boleslav the Cruel. Their mother, Drahomira, may also have been involved. She certainly had criminal form because apparently she had previously arranged for her mother-in-law, St Ludmila, to be strangled.

Although Wenceslas was not a king when he died, later in the tenth century he was posthumously styled Wenceslas I by Otto I, the Holy Roman Emperor. This has the potential to be confusing, because the real Wenceslaus I of Bohemia reigned in the thirteenth century. 'Good King' Wenceslas was later canonised and given the feast day of 28 September, which is said to be the day he died. He is now the patron saint of Bohemia, Prague and the Czech Republic. Wenceslas Square in Prague is named after him.

❧ The story of the carol ❧

There were all sorts of tales about Wenceslas's pious Christian nature. One of these is the belief that he would walk barefoot at night, with only his page for company, to distribute alms to the poor, and this story was commemorated in the carol that bears his name. The carol's lyrics were written by John Mason Neale, an Englishman, in 1853. They were set to the tune of 'Tempest Adest Floridum', one of the spring carols in the Finnish song collection 'Piae Cantiones', which was first published in 1582.

The words of the carol itself are a gift to children of every age. They have inspired corny jokes about Good King Wenceslas liking his pizzas 'deep and crisp and even', and schoolchildren stifle giggles when they sing 'heat was in the very sod which the saint had printed'. There is also the almost irresistible temptation to sing 'gathering winter few-*hew*-ell' instead of a more melodious rendition, no matter how often choirs are told not to do this.

THE FESTIVE FEAST

The fat boy took the opportunity of appropriating
for his own use, and summarily devouring, a
particularly fine mince-pie, that had been
carefully put by, for somebody else.

THE POSTHUMOUS PAPERS OF THE PICKWICK CLUB, CHARLES DICKENS

Bringing in the Boar's Head

The boar's head in hand bear I,
Bedecked with bays and rosemary;
And I pray you, my masters, be merry.

'The Boar's Head Carol'

The British countryside was once an unnerving and dangerous place. Yes, it could be bucolic and beautiful, but it was also the domain of hapless wild animals that were regarded with hostility by their human neighbours. Wolves, for instance, which were once a common sight in Britain, were so feared that they were eventually hunted to extinction. So, too, were the wild boar that once roamed the woods of the British Isles (and which have recently made a reappearance in the Forest of Dean and the East Sussex/Kent borders). These were regarded as vicious creatures, but they did have one thing in their favour – they made very good eating. So much so that they were once a centrepiece of the Christmas celebrations.

The tradition of serving a roasted boar's head during a feast held at the darkest time of the year is thought to be pre-Christian. One theory is that it is associated with the Norse god Freyr, who ruled farming and was often linked with a boar called Gullinbursti. Sacrificing and eating a boar during the winter solstice celebrations was a way of pleasing Freyr and ensuring that he took care of your livestock during the coming year. The Celts, on the other hand, believed that boars were evil creatures. When Christianity arrived in Britain, the tradition of roasting a boar's head at midwinter was reinterpreted and became symbolic of the victory of the Christ Child over sin and the powers of darkness.

Medieval Christmas celebrations including hunting for wild boar. When found, the animal was killed and carted off to the kitchen. The boar was roasted and its head was arranged on a silver platter and carried into the dining hall with great ceremony, accompanied by music and singing. This was known as 'bringing in the boar's head'. As the carol describes, the beast's head was decorated with greenery, including sprigs of bay leaves and rosemary.

Even though the tradition of bringing in the boar's head may have almost completely died out in most of Britain, it hasn't completely vanished. It is still upheld each year at Queen's College, Oxford, on or around 16 December. The story goes that the custom originated in 1340 when a student was ambling through a nearby Oxfordshire forest while reading a book by Aristotle. He was charged at by a wild boar and, lacking any other weapon, was quick-witted enough to ram his book into the open mouth of the marauding animal, which choked to death. Apparently, the cool-headed student even managed a quip, saying 'Graecum est', which means 'It's in Greek'.

The ceremony of bringing in the boar's head also continues in the City of London each December. The Worshipful Company of Cutlers has been celebrating the Feast of the Boar's Head, which is attended by the Lord Mayor of London and other dignitaries, since 1924, as part of their Christmas celebrations.

The carol quoted here is part of the one sung each year at Queen's College, but there are other carols about the boar's head as well. An early version of the Queen's College carol appeared in Wynken de Worde's first printed collection of carols in 1521.

A SIXTEENTH-CENTURY CHRISTMAS FEAST

Catering at Christmas can be a strenuous and expensive affair. The household accounts of the Duke of Buckingham's manor at Thornbury in Gloucestershire record not only the number and status of the people who ate their Christmas dinner there on 25 December 1507, but also the foods that were needed and how much they cost.

Dined 95 gentry, 107 yeoman, 97 garcons. Supped 84 gentry, 114 yeoman, 92 garcons.

Archates: 4 swans price 12s, 4 geese 2s, 5 suckling pigs 20d, 14 capons 8s, 18 chickens 18d, 21 rabbits 3/6d, 1 peacock 2s, 3 mallards 8d, 5 widgeons 10d, 12 teals 12d, 3 woodcocks 8d, 22 syntes [snipe] 12d, 12 large birds 3d, 400 hens eggs 3/4d, 2 dishes of butter 20d, 10 flagons of milk 10d, 1 flagon of rum 6d, 2 flagons of frumenty 4d, in herbs 1c

Kitchen spent of the Lord's store:
1 carcase and seven rounds of beef 20s
9 carcases of mutton price 16s
4 pigs 8s
1½ calves 4s

Cellar spent:
11 bottles and 3 quarts of Gascony wine price 13s
1½ pitchers of Rheinish wine price 15d
½ pitcher Malvoisey price 6d
butter
Spent in aile [ale] 171 flagons, 1 quart, price 13s 17½d

Having catered for a total of 589 guests on Christmas Day, the hard-working kitchen staff did it all again on 6 January (Twelfth Night, or the Feast of the Epiphany), when they fed 459 guests.

TWELFTH CAKE

In the days when Twelfth Night marked the last of the three extravagant feasts during the Twelve Days of Christmas, and before its popularity waned in Victorian times, it was celebrated in style. One of its central features was the Twelfth cake. This was a rich fruit cake and the predecessor of the Christmas cake that eventually overtook it in popularity.

In addition to the expected ingredients of dried fruits, eggs, flour, butter, sugar and spices, some other important items were stirred into the Twelfth cake mixture too. These were a bean, a pea and a clove. In an echo of the medieval and Tudor tradition of electing a Lord of Misrule to organise the Christmas festivities, whoever found the bean in their slice when the cake was cut on Twelfth Night became the King of the Bean. Whoever discovered the pea in their slice became the Queen of the Pea, and together they presided over the evening's entertainment. The person who found the clove became the Knave. At midnight, their rule ended and the world returned to normal.

Twelfth cakes were always highly and elaborately decorated, and by early Victorian times were usually made by bakers and confectioners, for whom this was their busiest time of year. Gradually, with the rise of Victorian prosperity, the peas and beans were replaced by silver trinkets, such as thimbles and rings. But the popularity of the Twelfth cake didn't last, and it waned in direct proportion to the growing preference for Christmas cakes that were served on Christmas Day. As for the silver trinkets, they eventually found their way into Victorian Christmas puddings ...

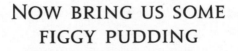

NOW BRING US SOME FIGGY PUDDING

One of the staples of the Christmas feast is the Christmas pudding – for those of us who like it. If its main ingredient of dried fruit puts you off, you might be even less enthusiastic about it if you were offered its culinary ancestors.

In medieval times, Christmas pudding was known as plum pottage, and was moist to the point of being sloppy. It had another distinction, too, because it contained diced beef or mutton as well as onions, dried fruit (hence the 'plum' in the name) and spices. This would have made it a very rich dish – in more ways than one, because you had to be fairly well off to be able to afford to make it.

The chopped meat, which has left an etymological ghost in the name of the sweet mincemeat that we now bake in mince pies, gradually vanished from the recipe and was replaced by shredded beef suet. The moisture content of the recipe was reduced until it had switched from being soft to solid. The pudding's name changed, too, and turned into plum or figgy pudding rather than pottage.

The Victorian version of plum pudding was quite dense, so it had to be boiled for several hours to make it edible, before being left to mature for a few days. It was boiled again on Christmas Day itself. Victorian illustrations of Christmas feasts often show perfectly spherical puddings, looking like large cannonballs, topped with a sprig of holly, but proud cooks liked to serve their puddings in special moulds too, as was the fashion of the time. Very often, Victorian cooks were much more interested in how their food looked than how it tasted. Regardless of the shape of the finished pudding, it would be brought into the dining room with tremendous ceremony, ablaze with brandy or rum. It was often served with a hot brandy-flavoured custard, or with what was then called hard sauce, but which we know now as brandy butter.

There was another treat to come, because tradition demanded that the cook had stirred a selection of trinkets or charms into the uncooked pudding. This was a throwback to the earlier tradition of the Twelfth cake, eaten on Twelfth Night. Diners would eat their portion of plum pudding carefully, so as not to choke on any trinket they might find in it. These trinkets caused great merriment because they were said to predict the recipient's fate. Pity the unmarried daughter of the house who found a silver thimble on her plate – it was deemed to indicate a long spinsterhood; or the young man who found a button in his pudding – it was a bachelor's button. But imagine how cheered you'd be if your spoonful yielded a silver sixpence (a sure sign of forthcoming riches) or a ring (marriage is on the way). You'd probably have to have a second helping just to celebrate, even if you had to go for a very long walk afterwards in the hope of digesting it all.

MINCE PIES

Like them or loathe them, mince pies are inseparable from the Christmas feast. We have been eating them for centuries, but not always in the form that we know them today, and we have not always called them by their current name, either.

Originally, as their contemporary name suggests, they contained meat. And not just any old meat – a recipe from 1394 advises the cook to mince up the flesh of one capon, one pheasant, one hare, two rabbits and two pigeons, to add the diced offal of all these creatures, plus plenty of seasoning, spice and stock, and to bake the lot in a huge pastry case. Other recipes combined meat with dried fruit. These mince pies were huge and expensive affairs, so were the preserve of the rich who had access to such a plentiful selection of fresh meat at a time of the year when it was generally in short supply. Less wealthy people adapted the recipe according to the contents of their larders.

Regardless of their ingredients, these pies were traditionally baked in large oblong dishes (which is why many pies of the time were called 'coffins' or 'coffyns'). These rich Christmas dishes were often called 'shred' (or 'shrid') pies, probably because they contained shredded meat. Some people knew them as mutton pies, presumably when that was their main ingredient, or as Christmas pies. Yet they soon gained what is to us the more familiar name of mince pies. It is said that their pastry covering often collapsed during the cooking process, making them look remarkably like cribs when they emerged from the oven. Apparently, for some people this conjured up a powerful association with the infant Jesus lying in the manger, and even inspired some bakers to garnish the pies with pastry babies.

This edible representation of Christ offended seventeenth-century Puritans, who felt it was superstitious and lost no time in condemning mince pies during the English Civil War. Mince pies became a secret and private indulgence.

Happily, Christmas returned when Charles II regained the throne in 1660, and mince pies could once again be eaten not only with relish but with impunity. However, they shrank after the Restoration; instead of being baked in a large dish they became individual, small pies often called wayfarer pies. Something else that changed was the meat content, which eventually dwindled to such an extent that only the suet was left. By the nineteenth century, Isabella Beeton, in her eponymous *Book of Household Management*, gave two recipes for mincemeat, one containing beef and the other without it.

Perhaps in an effort to introduce a Christian theme into mince pies, tradition dictates that the mincemeat mixture should contain three spices, as a reminder of the three gifts of gold, frankincense and myrrh given to the infant Jesus by the Magi. These spices are cinnamon, cloves and nutmeg.

'TAKE A LEGGE OF MUTTON'

This recipe for 'minc't pie' comes from *The English Huswife* by Gervase Markham, which was first published in 1615. As was the practice at the time, the recipe gives only general guidelines about the ingredients, because it was assumed that everyone knew how to cook and therefore had no need for detailed instructions.

Take a Legge of Mutton, and cut the best of the flesh from the bone, and parboyl it well then put to it three pound of the best Mutton suet & shred it very small; then spread it abroad, and fashion it with Salt Cloves and Mace: then put in good store of Currants, great Raisins and Prunes clean washed and picked a few Dates sliced, and some Orenge-pils sliced; then being all well mixt together, put it into a coffin, or divers coffins, and so bake them and when they are served up, open the lids and strow store of Sugar on the top of the meat and upon the lid. And in this sort you may also bake Beef or Veal, onely the Beef would not be parboyld, and the Veal will ask a double quantity of Suet.

Elizabeth Raffald included a recipe for 'mince pye' in her classic cookery book, *The Experienced English Housekeeper*, in 1784. In case you are wondering, a neat is an old-fashioned word for a horned cow or bull.

> Boil a neat's tongue two hours, then skin it, and chop it as small as possible, chop very small three pounds of fresh beef suet, three pounds of good baking apples, four pounds of currants clean washed, picked, and well dried before the fire, one pound of jar raisins stoned, and chopped small, and one pound of powder sugar, mix them all together with half an ounce of mace, the same of nutmeg grated, cloves and cinnamon a quarter of an ounce of each, and one pint of French Brandy, and make a rich puff paste; as you fill the pye up, put in a little candied citron and orange cut in little pieces, what you have to spare; put close down in a pot and cover it up, put no citron or orange in till you use it.

A Yorkshire Christmas pye

Standing pies were massive and complex affairs, the ingredients encased within a thick pastry crust. This crust wasn't intended to be eaten; it merely acted as a support for all the foodstuffs it encased. Each diner discarded their portion of the crust when the 'pye' was served. Today, we know standing pies better as raised pies, and make them with a hot water pastry that is far too delicious to throw away. A classic example of this sort of pie is a traditionally made pork pie.

Although the following recipe seems over-elaborate, not to say completely over the top, to our contemporary eyes (and stomachs), it was a popular dish for those who could afford it. The recipe was written by Hannah Glasse, and appeared in her book *The Art of Cookery Made Plain and Easy*, c.1747.

First make a good Standing Crust, let the Wall and Bottom be very thick, bone a Turkey, a Goose, a Fowl, a Partridge, and a Pigeon, season them all very well, take half an Ounce of Mace, half an Ounce of Nutmegs, a quarter of an Ounce of Cloves, half an Ounce of black Pepper, all beat fine together, two large Spoonfuls of Salt, mix them together. Open the Fowls, then the Goose, and then the Turkey, which must be large; season them all well first, and lay them in the Crust, so as it will look only like a whole Turkey; then have a hare ready cased, and wiped with a clean Cloth. Cut it to Pieces, that is jointed; season it, and lay it as close as you can on one Side; on the other Side Woodcock, more Game, and what Sort of wild Fowl you can get. Season them well, and lay them close; put at least four Pounds of Butter into the Pye, then lay on your Lid, which must be a very thick one, and let it be well baked. It must have a very hot Oven, and will take at least four Hours. This Pye will take a Bushel of Flour; in this Chapter you will see how to make it. These Pies are often sent to London in a Box as Presents; therefore the Walls must be well built.

THE LONG WALK

No one in Europe knew what a turkey was until the sixteenth century, when Spanish explorers sailed to the Americas and took some of the exotic creatures they found there back to Europe.

One of these was the turkey, and it is thought that the first members of this extravagantly plumed species arrived in Britain in 1526, brought by a Yorkshire navigator called William Strickland. Their arrival was such a success that when Strickland was granted a coat of arms in 1550, they included the image of a turkey. The story goes that Henry VIII – never one to turn down a square meal – was the first Briton to eat a turkey.

❧ A rich dish ❧

These birds were called turkeys because merchants from the Levant first sold them into Britain, so their name was a description of the merchants' origins. The birds made succulent eating but, even after their high price had been halved by the 1570s, they were still the preserve of the rich. Poor people could only dream of eating them.

Turkeys had become part of the well-heeled (and belt-bursting) British Christmas feast by 1585, according to Thomas Tusser's *Five Hundred Points of Good Husbandry*:

> Beefe, mutton, and pork, shred pies of the best,
> Pig, veal, goose, and capon, and turkey well drest;
> Cheese, apples, and nuts, jolly carols to hear,
> As then in the country is counted good cheer.

Norfolk in East Anglia was (and still is) a particularly good breeding place for turkeys. In fact, the Norfolk black turkey is thought to be Britain's oldest breed. These birds became particularly popular in Victorian times, gradually overtaking both beef and geese as the favoured choice for Christmas dinner for those that could afford them, and the London markets did a roaring trade. In Charles Dickens's *A Christmas Carol*, Scrooge watches the impoverished Cratchit family making the best of their meagre Christmas dinner of roast goose and, at the end of the story, sends them a turkey so large that 'he never could have stood upon his legs, that bird. He would have snapped 'em off short in a minute, like sticks of sealing-wax'.

✎ Getting the birds to market ✎

The breeders had to transport the birds from Norfolk to the metropolis, and the easiest way to do that was to accompany them on foot on what was always a very long tramp. The turkeys, their feet tarred to protect them from the hard roads, were marched down south each October. When they and their drover reached London, they had to take byways and side streets to avoid being trampled under horse-drawn carriages. By the time they arrived the turkeys were decidedly more svelte than when they'd set off, even though they grazed on the fields they passed along the way, so it was essential that there was plenty of time for the exhausted, hungry and dehydrated creatures to be fattened up again. After all, who in their right mind would want to spend good money on a scrawny turkey come Christmas?

A FESTIVE MENU

Mrs Isabella Beeton was the doyenne and guide for many cooks and housewives in the Victorian era. Her celebrated *Mrs Beeton's Book of Household Management* was crammed with useful information on everything from how to treat a nosebleed to the German method of cooking turnips (simmered in broth, in case you are wondering). In the 1869 edition of her book (published four years after her death in childbirth and edited by her publisher husband), she suggests a 'bill of fare' for a December dinner for ten people.

How women diners coped with such a massive array of food while wearing tightly laced corsets is nothing short of a marvel.

First course
Mulligatawny soup
Fried slices of codfish
Soles à la crème

Entrées
Croquettes of fowl
Pork cutlets and tomato sauce

Second course
Roast ribs of beef
Boiled turkey and celery sauce
Tongue, garnished
Lark pudding
Vegetables

Third course
Roast hare
Grouse
Plum pudding
Mince pies
Charlotte à la Parisienne
Cheesecakes
Apple tart
Nesselrode pudding

Desserts and ices

TRADITIONAL SCOTTISH FOODS

Many traditional foods have been forgotten or lost, but less so in Scotland. Here are some foods that have been served there either at Christmas or Hogmanay for centuries.

❧ Bannocks ❧

A bannock is a type of oatcake, originally made from oatmeal mixed with water or milk, and baked on a girdle or griddle. Special bannocks were made to celebrate Christmas and Hogmanay, and were usually eaten with sheep's cheese. They might also be served with caudle, a hot drink made from eggs, milk, oatmeal, whisky or ale and spices. Today, bannocks are more likely to be made from wheatmeal rather than oatmeal.

❧ Black bun ❧

One of the staple foods of a Scottish Christmas is black bun. It is a rich fruit cake, wrapped in a pastry case, that was once eaten on Twelfth Night but is now more usually consumed at Hogmanay. The cake is similar to a rich Christmas cake, being made from many of the same ingredients, but one difference is that it contains ground ginger and black pepper. Like a Christmas cake, black bun should be made several weeks in advance, to allow the cake to mature, and stored in an airtight container until ready to eat.

❧ Clootie dumpling ❧

The clootie dumpling is a Scottish cousin of the Christmas pudding. They have several ingredients in common, including dried fruit, flour, breadcrumbs, suet and spices, and they are both traditionally wrapped in cloth ('clootie', also spelt 'cloutie', is a Scots word for 'cloth') and boiled for several hours. And the generous cook may also feel inspired to stir some coins into both puddings, especially when they will be served on Christmas Day. For many people, though, the clootie dumpling belongs to Hogmanay. Others are happy to eat it whenever they get the chance, regardless of what the calendar says.

The dry ingredients for a clootie dumpling are mixed together before being moistened with milk, and sometimes golden syrup, and wrapped in a large, floured muslin cloth. The dumpling boils merrily in a big saucepan for its allotted time of roughly three hours. Then it's removed from the pan, left until the muslin can be handled without fear of getting third-degree burns, and unwrapped. You might want to eat it at this stage. Alternatively, if you are following tradition and not yet starving hungry, you put it on a plate and leave it to dry before the fire, or put it on a baking sheet and let it dry in the oven. When the moment finally comes to eat the dumpling, it is delicious served with cream, custard, ice cream or possibly even all three, if you're in the mood.

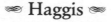

∽ Haggis ∽

Robert Burns so memorably called it 'Chieftain o' the puddin-race', and generations of Scots, as well as Burns fans of other nationalities, eat it on Burns Night (25 January) to commemorate the great poet's birthday. But haggis (which may or may not have originated in Scotland – no one has the definitive answer to this) is eaten at other times of the year as well, including Christmas and Hogmanay.

Haggis is a classic reminder that meat was once highly prized by many people, who therefore had to use every scrap of an animal that they could. Nothing went to waste. Originally, haggis was made from a sheep's heart, liver and lights (lungs), which were minced up and mixed with oatmeal, chopped onion, suet and seasonings, then sewn into the sheep's stomach. The haggis was boiled for several hours and often served with neeps and tatties (mashed swede and mashed potatoes, served separately) or clap-shot (neeps and tatties mashed together with butter and plenty of chopped chives).

∾ Skeachan cake ∾

This is similar to black bun, but without the pastry casing. It is made from dried fruit that has been steeped in ale and black treacle for twenty-four hours, plus butter, sugar, eggs and flour, and spices that include plenty of ginger. Skeachan itself, from which the cake gets its name, is a type of treacle ale that was once drunk over the Christmas period.

A RIGHT ROYAL CHRISTMAS DINNER

Here is the menu for Queen Victoria's Christmas dinner in 1899. It was written in French, as was customary at the time, although some English words were used when there was no French equivalent, such as the very English accompaniment to the turkey (described here as 'dinde').

Potages

Consommé à la Monaco [consomme with spring
vegetables and truffles]
Du Berry [consomme with cauliflower]

Poissons

Fillet of Sole à la Vassant

Eperlans frits [fried smelts], sauce Verneuil

Entrée

Cotelettes de Volaille [chicken breasts] à la York

Relevés

Dinde à la Chipolata [turkey with chipolatas]

Roast Beef

Chine of Pork

Entremets

Asperges [asparagus], sauce Hollandaise

Mince pies

Plum pudding

Gelée d'orange l'anglaise [orange jelly]

Buffet

Baron of beef

Boar's head

Game pie

Woodcock pie

Brawn

Roast fowl

Tongue

It is interesting to compare this with the menu served at Sandringham on 25 December 1930 to King George V, Queen Mary and the other members of the Royal Family. This menu is much simpler, but times were harder, too.

Clear soup

Fried fillets of sole

Braised York ham

Roast Norfolk turkey, stuffed with chestnuts

Lettuce salad

Cauliflower soufflé

Plum pudding

Mince pies

CHRISTMAS COOKERY

Christmas is the season for kindling the fire of
hospitality in the hall, the genial flame of charity
in the heart.

OLD CHRISTMAS, WASHINGTON IRVING

PERFECT POTATOES

For many of us, one of the great joys of Christmas is all the tempting leftovers that sit in the fridge or larder, just begging to be eaten. There is an unproven theory that when food is eaten standing up it is free of both calories and carbohydrates. Some of us hope this is especially true of food eaten surreptitiously, such as when you are supposed to be doing the washing up but you simply can't resist polishing off that lonely roast potato with a dollop of bread sauce smeared on top of it.

However, sometimes those leftovers develop a reproachful air. 'Why haven't you eaten me yet?' they demand whenever you open the fridge to get out some cream for yet another mince pie. (After all, it is supposed to be lucky to eat lots of them at Christmas.) A delicious side dish can make all the difference to yet another plate of cold turkey or ham, and this simple recipe for potatoes certainly fits the bill. It is also good with many other meats, as well as hot or cold quiches. When preparing the potatoes, it is best to slice them as thinly as possible, so they cook more quickly.

Serves 4 people

50 g (2 oz) butter, plus extra for greasing
15 ml (1 tbsp) olive oil
2 medium onions, peeled and sliced
2 cloves of garlic, peeled and chopped
3 sticks of celery, trimmed and finely sliced
2 large leeks, trimmed and finely sliced
1.3 kg (3 lb) potatoes, thinly sliced
800 ml (27 fl oz) hot vegetable stock
5 g (1 tsp) English mustard
5 ml (1 tsp) dried thyme
salt and black pepper

Butter a deep baking dish, roughly 24 x 30 cm (9½ x 12 in), and preheat the oven to 200°C/400°F/Gas Mark 6. Melt the butter and oil in a large frying pan, then add the sliced onions, garlic, celery and leeks and cook on a low heat, stirring occasionally, for about 10 minutes or until soft but not brown. Remove from the heat. Spread one-third of this vegetable mixture over the bottom of the baking dish. Now arrange one-third of the sliced potatoes on top, and season well with salt and freshly ground black pepper. Repeat with two more layers of the vegetables, potatoes and seasoning, finishing with the potatoes. Place the baking dish on a baking sheet.

Put the mustard and thyme in a measuring jug and pour on the hot vegetable stock, stirring well. Pour this over the potatoes until it reaches three-quarters up the sides of the baking dish. Save the rest in case it is needed later. Dot the top layer with small pieces of butter and bake for about 1 hour, or until the potatoes are tender (test those in the middle of the baking dish as well as the edges) and the top is golden. Tuck a sheet of aluminium foil over the baking dish if the potatoes are becoming too brown. This also helps to cook the potatoes more quickly by steaming them. Check the dish occasionally to ensure it is still moist, and top up with the remaining stock if it gets too dry.

BREAD SAUCE

There is always so much to prepare for the Christmas feast (or feasts, if you're lucky) that it's tempting to save time by buying some ready-made foods, especially when it comes to bread sauce. But home-made bread sauce, when properly made, is a completely different beast to the stuff that comes out of a packet, and once eaten you will be unlikely to want to return to the convenience variety.

As with so many recipes, the quality of the ingredients will affect the finished result. Ideally, use whole milk or Jersey milk for its creamy texture and taste. And, equally importantly, use a good-quality white bread that is a day or two old (when it is easier to turn it into bread-crumbs). Cheap sliced bread will give very disappointing results, assuming you can manage to make breadcrumbs (rather than bread pills) in the first place.

If you are pushed for time on Christmas Day, as most of us are, you can prepare the bread sauce the day before and leave it in the fridge, then reheat and finish it on the day. Alternatively, you can make it up to a month in advance and freeze it – but don't forget to defrost it in good time!

Serves 6–8 people

1 medium onion, peeled
4 cloves
570 ml (1 pint) whole or Jersey milk
4 black peppercorns
1 bay leaf
175 g (6 oz) fresh white breadcrumbs
salt to taste
freshly grated nutmeg
25 g (1 oz) butter
55 ml (2 fl oz) double cream

Cut the onion in half and stud each half with two cloves. Pour the milk into a large saucepan and add the onion halves, the peppercorns and the bay leaf. Leave on a low heat until the milk starts to simmer, then take the pan off the heat and set aside for at least 30 minutes to allow the onions, bay leaf and spices to infuse the milk. Strain the liquid into a clean saucepan, add the breadcrumbs, salt and grated nutmeg and stir over a gentle heat until the sauce has thickened. Stir in the butter and cream, and cook for another 3 minutes. Spoon into a warmed serving dish and drape a sheet of greaseproof paper directly on top of the bread sauce to stop it forming a skin.

If you are making this well ahead of time, take it off the heat after you have thickened it with breadcrumbs. Store it in the fridge in a sealed container, with the top of the sauce covered with greaseproof paper. When you are ready to finish it, spoon it into a saucepan, gently heat it and stir in the butter and cream.

It is unlikely that there will be any leftovers.

~~~~~~~~~

A GOOD ROASTING

According to 'The Christmas Song', which was written by Mel Tormé and Bob Wells in 1946, chestnuts roasting on an open fire are an essential part of Christmas. So, if you want the full festive experience, you should forget about buying them vacuum-packed or frozen for easy cooking, and buy whole raw nuts.

When buying loose chestnuts, which are available in Britain from late September until late December, you should choose nuts that are plump, smooth and shiny because they will make the best eating. Shun any nuts that are wizened or smelly, as they will taste horrid. On no account should you confuse edible chestnuts (*Castanea* sp.) with the inedible horse chestnuts (*Aesculus* sp.) with which children play conkers in the autumn.

Once you've got the edible chestnuts home, you can treat them in several different ways. However, you must bear in mind that nature gave chestnuts an almost impenetrable suit of armour – their outer shells are hard and therefore need special treatment before you can take things any further.

The first item you need is a sharp knife (and the sharper the better) so you can make a small cut in the outer shell of each nut, to stop it bursting open during the cooking process. A blunt knife could slip on the shell, with the result that the second item you will need is a packet of sticking plasters. This tends to cast a blight over the cosy Christmassy feel you are trying to evoke, so is best avoided.

❧ Water, water ❧

In her seminal work, *Modern Cookery for Private Families* (first published in Britain in 1845), Eliza Acton gives a recipe for chestnuts that are boiled for up to an hour until soft, dried and then eaten. For roasted chestnuts, she recommends par-boiling them in plenty of salted water for about ten minutes before drying them in a cloth and roasting them in the oven or over an open fire.

❧ Roasting over an open fire ❧

Ideally, you should use a special chestnut roasting pan, which has small holes in its base and a very long handle so you can avoid roasting yourself as well as the chestnuts. Alternatively, you can use a cast-iron frying pan, but hold it while wearing a thick oven glove to protect your hand from the heat. You also need a small sharp knife and a clean tea towel. Finally, make sure you have a comfortable chair and maybe a good book.

All you do is arrange the chestnuts in the pan, sit in the chair and hold the pan over the roaring hot fire, taking care not to singe your hands in the process. Give the chestnuts a little shake every now and then, preferably taking the pan out of the fire so you can easily rescue any chestnuts that go overboard. Start testing the chestnuts when they have turned black, after about 20–25 minutes. The shell will have begun to open at the point where you cut it, and you can carefully push the blade of a knife into the centre of the chestnut. If it goes in easily, the chestnut is cooked. If it doesn't, return the pan to the fire for a few more minutes and then try again.

When they're ready, tip the chestnuts into the tea towel and leave them to cool down for about 10 minutes, then peel off the outer casing and the inner pith, and eat them.

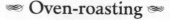

❧ Oven-roasting ❧

If you don't have an open fire, you can easily roast the chestnuts in the oven. This certainly reduces the discomfort of leaning over a hot fire but it also reduces the old-fashioned Christmassy atmosphere of the whole enterprise. Preheat the oven to 225°C/425°F/Gas Mark 7, arrange the chestnuts on a baking sheet and roast for about 30 minutes or until cooked. Then leave the chestnuts to cool, as when roasting on the fire, before eating them.

❧ Easy peel ❧

Chestnuts are much easier to peel when they are warm than when they are cold, so it is wise to peel the entire batch of roasted chestnuts even if you don't want to eat them all in one sitting.

HARD SAUCE!

We have been putting a buttery, sugary and brandy-laced confection on our plum puddings and mince pies for many

Christmases. Our Victorian ancestors called it hard sauce (which makes it sound like the sort of consolatory expression you might find in a PG Wodehouse novel – 'I say, hard sauce, old chap!') but we know it as brandy butter.

If you don't care for brandy, you can use rum instead or any suitable liqueur, such as Cointreau. You will notice the difference in taste if you use the best butter you can buy. On no account be tempted to cut financial corners and use margarine.

Ideally, brandy butter should be made at least twenty-four hours ahead and kept in the fridge or larder, to give the flavours time to develop.

110 g (4 oz) unsalted butter, softened
110 g (4 oz) icing sugar, sifted
15 ml (1 tbsp) brandy, rum or liqueur

Cream the butter until it has become pale and soft. Gradually incorporate the icing sugar, stirring it in carefully at first to avoid it blowing in every direction. Add the alcohol in small doses to prevent the mixture curdling. Taste it and add some more alcohol if necessary.

BRANDY CREAM

If you fancy being completely indulgent over Christmas and putting pretty much everything except the kitchen sink on your mince pies, brandy cream is a must. It is also an excellent alternative to hard sauce, aka brandy butter, if you find that too sweet.

You can buy tubs of ready-made brandy cream in supermarkets but it is much cheaper to make it yourself, provided that you have the brandy ready and waiting in a cupboard. If brandy isn't to your taste, you could use a suitable liqueur instead, such as Drambuie or Grand Marnier.

300 ml (9 fl oz) double cream
25 g (1 oz) icing sugar, sifted
30 ml (2 tbsp) brandy or liqueur

Put the cream, icing sugar and brandy or liqueur in a bowl and whip until the mixture forms soft peaks. Leave it in the fridge, covered, until ready to serve.

CHOCOLATE TRUFFLES

What could be better at the end of a meal than a chocolate truffle? Two of them, perhaps?

Home-made chocolate truffles are ideal gifts, especially if you package them beautifully in plenty of transparent wrapping paper or a pretty box. Some recipes for chocolate truffles are very complicated but this one is simplicity itself.

For the best results, choose a good-quality dark chocolate. Any chocolate containing at least 70 per cent cocoa solids needs careful handling because it can split as it melts, leaving you with thick chocolate underneath and a top layer of oil. You may get better results from chocolate with a slightly lower percentage of cocoa solids.

This is a three-way recipe. As soon as it's ready you can pour it over ice cream; you can leave it to cool, when it becomes chocolate ganache to spread over a Yule log; or you can turn it into truffles, as described here.

200 ml (7 fl oz) double cream
200 g (7 oz) good-quality plain chocolate, broken into pieces
brandy, rum or liqueur (optional)
instant coffee granules (optional)
zest of an unwaxed orange (optional)
chopped nuts (optional)
cocoa powder, sifted (optional)

melted plain, milk or white chocolate (optional)
individual foil or paper sweet cases (optional)

Warm the double cream in a milk saucepan until it begins to steam. On no account let it boil. Take it off the heat and stir in the broken chocolate pieces until they have melted. Return the pan to the heat and stir until the mixture is just coming to the boil. Remove from the heat.

If you are making one large batch of plain chocolate truffles, put the saucepan in a cool place until the mixture has set. Alternatively, if you are making a selection of differently flavoured truffles, divide the mixture between the requisite number of bowls.

For coffee truffles, dissolve 10 g (2 tsp) instant coffee granules in a tiny amount of boiling water and stir into the truffle mixture. Add a splash of brandy, rum or a liqueur if you wish. Stir, cover and leave to set in a cool place.

For brandy or rum truffles, stir in the brandy or rum a teaspoon at a time until you reach the desired strength. Stir, cover and leave to set in a cool place.

For orange truffles, grate the zest of an unwaxed orange into the truffle mixture. Stir, cover and leave to set in a cool place.

When the mixture has set, scoop out small amounts either with a teaspoon or a melon baller. Quickly roll each truffle between your palms and place on a sheet of greaseproof paper. When all the truffles are ready, you can dip them in melted chocolate and leave them to set on a sheet of baking parchment, or you can roll them in chopped nuts or in sifted cocoa powder. Leave them in a cool place to set.

You can place some of the truffles in individual foil or paper sweet cases, or leave them as they are, before packing them in boxes or individual clear wrap bags.

PEPPERMINT CREAMS

These are wonderfully moreish and they make great Christmas presents – assuming that they will last long enough for you to wrap them. When wrapping up home-made edible gifts, presentation is key. You can put these peppermint creams in see-through bags tied with pretty ribbon, or arrange them in an old chocolate box that you've re-covered with Christmas wrapping paper and lined with white tissue paper.

If you've made too much royal icing for your Christmas cake, you can simply add a few drops of peppermint extract to the spare icing. Alternatively, you can make the peppermint creams from scratch.

Makes about 20 sweets

1 egg white
400 g (14 oz) icing sugar, sifted, plus more for dusting
5 ml (1 tsp) peppermint extract
150 g (5 oz) plain chocolate (optional)

Place the egg white in a spotlessly clean bowl (any grease will stop it frothing up) and whisk until the white stands up in peaks. Slowly whisk in the icing sugar and peppermint extract to form a stiff paste. Taste to check the flavour and add a little more peppermint extract if necessary.

Sift some icing sugar on to a clean board and roll out the peppermint paste to a thickness of about 5 mm (¼ in). Cut out the peppermint creams using small cutters in Christmassy shapes, and arrange on a baking sheet lined with baking parchment. Leave in a warmish place to dry overnight.

You can leave the peppermint creams unadorned. Alternatively, you can decorate some of them with melted plain chocolate. Break up the chocolate into small pieces and melt it in a bowl above a pan of hot water. Now dip the peppermint creams in the chocolate. You can immerse them fully, half-dip them or drizzle trails of chocolate over them. Leave them to set on a baking sheet lined with baking parchment.

CHRISTMAS CAKE

Some people love a rich fruit cake, dense with dried fruit and fragrant with brandy and spices. Others prefer something lighter, which is not only easier to digest but does not have to be made so far in advance. This is a perfect recipe for a cake that isn't as heavy as a traditional Christmas cake but is still special, thanks to the ground almonds it contains.

350 g (12 oz) butter
350 g (12 oz) light brown muscovado sugar
350 g (12 oz) plain flour, sifted
20 ml (4 tsp) baking powder, sifted
6 eggs, beaten
200 g (8 oz) mixed peel
200 g (8 oz) raisins
200 g (8 oz) sultanas
200 g (8 oz) currants
200 g (8 oz) ground almonds
10 ml (2 tsp) mixed spice
5 ml (1 tsp) cinnamon
5 ml (1 tsp) grated nutmeg
grated zest of 2 lemons
30 ml (2 tbsps) milk

Preheat the oven to 170°C/375°F/Gas Mark 3. Prepare a 28 cm (11 in) round cake tin or 25.5 cm (10 in) square cake tin by lining its base and sides with baking parchment. In a large bowl, cream together the butter and sugar until very soft. Sift the flour and baking powder into a separate bowl. Add the eggs to the butter and sugar mixture one at a time, adding a little of the sifted flour with the second and third egg to prevent the mixture curdling. Stir the mixed peel, raisins, sultanas, currants, ground almonds, spices and lemon zest into the bowl of flour and baking powder, then fold this mixture into the batter a little at a time. Stir in the milk until the mixture is soft and moist but not wet. Mix well, then spoon the cake mixture into the prepared cake tin. Protect the cake from over-baking by tying a thick collar of newspaper around the outside of the tin. Bake in the middle of the oven for 2–2½ hours, or until a clean skewer inserted into the cake comes out clean. If the top of the cake starts to colour too deeply, protect it with a sheet of greaseproof paper. Ovens vary in their cooking time, so check the cake before the time is up in case it has finished cooking.

Remove the cake from the oven and leave to cool in its tin before turning it on to a wire cooling rack and peeling off the baking parchment. Wrap it in greaseproof paper and then in a layer of aluminium foil, and store in an airtight tin for two weeks. The cake can be eaten undecorated, or can be decorated with a layer of marzipan and royal icing.

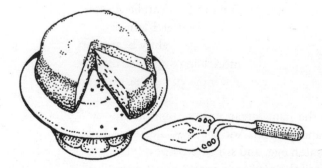

MMM, MARZIPAN

Home-made marzipan is delicious and surprisingly easy to make. It is less sweet than many shop-bought marzipans, and its delectable almond flavour is the perfect partner to Christmas cake.

If you want a perfectly smooth iced top to your cake – and assuming that there were no disasters such as a corner of the cake getting stuck to the side of the tin – you can turn the cake upside down so that what was the bottom becomes the flat top. When you have covered the cake with the marzipan you must leave it to dry out for at least 24 hours before icing it.

If you have any marzipan left over after you've covered your cake, you can make small sweets by dipping little pieces of marzipan in melted dark chocolate and leaving them to set on baking parchment.

This makes enough to ice a 28 cm (11 in) round cake
or a 25.5 cm (10 in) square cake

225 g (8 oz) unrefined icing sugar, sifted
225 g (8 oz) unrefined caster sugar
450 g (1 lb) ground almonds
5 ml (1 tsp) vanilla essence
juice of 1 lemon
2 eggs, lightly beaten
more icing sugar for dusting
apricot jam, sieved

Place the icing sugar, caster sugar and ground almonds in a large bowl and stir well. Add the vanilla essence and lemon juice, plus half the beaten egg, and stir to incorporate. Continue to add the beaten egg until the marzipan forms a stiff paste. Roll it into a ball.

Dust a clean flat surface with icing sugar. Cut the marzipan ball in two and roll out one half into a long strip until about 6 mm (¼ in) thick. Roll it into a square or a circle, according to the shape of the cake. Brush the top of the Christmas cake (which was originally the bottom) with the sieved apricot jam, then hold it by its sides and turn it upside down on to the middle of the marzipan. Turn it back on to its base and gently smooth over the top. Now roll out the rest of the marzipan into a long strip for the sides. Brush apricot jam over the sides of the cake, then press the long strip around them. Trim the joins with a knife, smooth them over with your fingertips and use offcuts of marzipan to fill any gaps.

Cover the cake with a clean tea towel and leave in a cool place for at least 24 hours before icing it.

THE ICING ON THE CAKE

Whether you like beautifully smooth white icing that resembles a perfectly ironed sheet, or a roughed-up surface that looks more like edible Artex, the Christmas cake doesn't seem finished until it's been suitably decorated. You can adorn it with old plaster favourites that take you back to your childhood, such as postboxes, robins and Father Christmases in long red coats, or you can opt for something much more contemporary, but it's the taste of the cake that's most important. And if the icing is too sweet or rock-hard, it will spoil the cake it encloses.

Royal icing is the traditional icing for a Christmas cake. You can beat it by hand if you're feeling energetic, but it is much quicker to use a food processor. Even if you normally use unrefined sugar for baking, you will have to switch to refined icing sugar for this recipe in order to get a very white icing.

This makes enough to ice a 28 cm (11 in) round cake or a 25.5 cm (10 in) square cake

2 egg whites
450 g (1 lb) icing sugar, sifted
10 ml (2 tsp) lemon juice
5 ml (1 tsp) glycerine

Make sure the bowl and its beater, or your wooden spoon, are completely clean and free of grease. Place all the ingredients in the bowl and beat them together. Go slowly at first, to avoid filling the room with clouds of icing sugar, then increase your speed. Beat the icing until it is smooth, white and thick, and stands up in peaks. Cover it with a clean damp tea towel and leave for one hour, so any air bubbles can rise to the surface, before spreading it on the marzipan-covered cake.

NOT A TRIFLING MATTER

One of the great joys of the Christmas feast is the opportunity to eat all sorts of foods that might be on the banned list, for calorific reasons, during the rest of the year. It is also a wonderful chance to eat lots of comfortingly familiar dishes which evoke a warm glow of nostalgia, not to mention happy tummies all round. ('Round' may be the operative word here.)

Trifle is one of those nostalgic dishes. An object of fear and loathing for some, an occasion of lavish indulgence for others, trifle can arouse heartfelt and heated passions. Some of us still remember, with a barely repressed shudder, those rock-solid conglomerations of over-sweet jelly, gritty half-dissolved sponge, tinned fruit cocktail, rubbery custard and synthetic cream, topped with a hectic sprinkling of hundreds and thousands or possibly a criss-cross of bright green angelica and scarlet glacé cherries. The sort of trifle that wouldn't quiver even if you held it upside down and jiggled it about. Some of us, it must be said, still love this sort of trifle that has to be chewed quite hard before it can be safely swallowed. Is this what Shakespeare meant when he wrote of 'a snapper-up of ill-considered trifles'?

Here is a recipe for anyone who prefers their Christmas trifle to be rather more on the wobbly side. It can be made almost entirely from scratch, if there is time, using home-made Madeira cake, egg custard and that compote of summer fruits you so thoughtfully bottled in readiness, many months ago. Alternatively, you can buy all the ingredients (buying the very best you can afford will make all the difference) and no one will raise even the hint of an eyebrow. They will be far too busy eyeing up what's left in the bowl and wondering if they can squeeze in another helping without looking like a complete pig.

Although you can make trifle in any sort of serving dish at a pinch, it is at its most mouthwatering and delectable if it's made in a glass bowl. And the more decorative the bowl, the better. This is an opportunity to dig out the cut-glass bowl that's been languishing at the back of a cupboard for years, carefully wash it in warm soapy water and buff it dry until it sparkles. The trifle is best if made at least twenty-four hours in advance, so the flavours have time to develop.

Serves 6–8 people

1 Madeira cake
600 g (1 lb 5 oz) cherry compote
45 ml (3 tbsp) French brandy or Oloroso sherry
500 ml (17 fl oz) fresh vanilla custard
300 ml (8 fl oz) double cream, whipped until it forms thick peaks
flaked almonds or dark chocolate curls to decorate

Cut the Madeira cake in half lengthwise, then cut widthwise into slices about 1 cm (½ in) thick. Put a spoonful of the cherry compote in the bottom of the glass bowl and place a single layer of the cake on top of it. Drizzle on some of the brandy or sherry – the aim is to flavour the cake with the alcohol but not drench it so it falls apart. Leave for a few minutes, then spoon on a layer of the cherry compote, followed by another layer of cake, and then the brandy or sherry. Continue until you have used up all the cake and compote, ending with a layer of cake, which should be as flat as you can make it. Pour on the custard, smoothing the top with a palette knife. Now spoon on the whipped cream, either spreading it into a thick layer or leaving it in decorative spoonfuls. Finish by decorating the top of the trifle with flaked almonds or curls of dark chocolate. Cover with clingfilm and store in the fridge. Allow it to come to room temperature roughly 30 minutes before serving. And don't be surprised if it all disappears in one sitting.

CHEERS!

'Tis not the drinking that is to be blamed,
but the excess.

TABLE TALK: HUMILITY, JOHN SELDEN

POSSET

The winter months are a good time to experiment with all sorts of hot drinks. Many of the drinks that were comfortingly familiar to our ancestors have fallen out of fashion or almost disappeared altogether, and are worth reviving.

Posset is one of them. It is a mixture of hot milk curdled with some form of alcohol and then spiced, and was very popular between the fifteenth and nineteenth centuries.

This is Hannah Glasse's recipe, with its original spelling (or 'fpelling', if you prefer) for 'an excellent sack-poffet'. It comes from her book *The Art of Cookery Made Plain and Easy*, first published in 1796.

Beat fifteen eggs, whites and yolks very well, and ftrain them; then put three quarters of a pound of white fugar into a pint of canary [a sweet wine from the Canary Islands, similar to Madeira], and mix it with your eggs in a bafon; fet it over a chafing-difh of coals, and keep continually ftirring it till it is fcalding hot; in the meantime grate fome nutmeg in a quart of milk and boil it; then pour it into your eggs and wine, they being fcalding hot: hold your hand very high as you pour it, and fomebody ftirring it all the time you are pouring in the milk;

then take it off the chafing-difh, fet it before the fire half an hour, and ferve it up.

HET PINT

A century or more ago, when first-footers were out at Hogmanay, they carried toddy kettles, made of copper, which were full of het pint ('hot pint'). Whenever they met anyone out on their travels, they would offer him or her a cup of the het pint, plus a toast to a good new year. Anyone who refused to drink the het pint was considered to be a miserable old curmudgeon.

110 g (4 oz) sugar
2.4 litres (4 pints) mild ale
5 ml (1 tsp) grated nutmeg
3 eggs, beaten
285 ml (½ pint) whisky

Dissolve the sugar in a little of the cold ale and set to one side. Pour the ale into a large saucepan, grate in the nutmeg, and heat until it is just coming to the boil. In the meantime, warm some tankards or large jugs. Stir in the sugary ale and take the saucepan off the heat. Pour in the beaten egg in a very slow trickle while continually stirring to stop the mixture curdling. Pour in the whisky, then heat the mixture again, still stirring it, but don't let it boil.

Pour the mixture back and forth between the saucepan and the heated tankards or jugs until it is clear and smooth. It is now ready to drink.

A GLASS OF BISHOP

Bishop (sometimes known as 'smoking bishop') was once a very popular winter drink. Here is Eliza Acton's recipe from *Modern Cookery for Private Families*, first published in 1845. She recommended substituting a Seville orange for the lemon because, she said, it tasted 'infinitely finer'.

Make several incisions in the rind of a lemon, stick cloves in these, and roast the lemon by a slow fire. Put small but equal quantities of cinnamon, cloves, mace and allspice, with a race of ginger [ginger root], into a saucepan with half a pint of water; let it boil until it is reduced one-half. Boil one bottle of port wine, burn a portion of the spirit out of it by applying a lighted paper to the saucepan; put the roasted lemon and spice into the wine; stir it up well, and let it stand near the fire ten minutes. Rub a few knobs of sugar on the rind of a lemon, put the sugar into a bowl or jug, with the juice of half a lemon (not roasted), pour the wine into it, grate in some nutmeg, sweeten it to the taste, and serve it up with the lemon and spice floating in it.

DR JOHNSON'S MULLED WINE

Dr Samuel Johnson, that celebrated (or notorious, depending on your point of view) man of letters, was said to be a big fan of mulled wine, and particularly of this recipe.

The success of this recipe is determined by the quality of the wine you use. Choose the best quality wine you can afford and don't be tempted to use the dubious-looking bottle that you won in a raffle. If it's rot-gut when it's cold, unfortunately it will still be rot-gut when it's hot.

Makes about 1.6 litres (2¾ pints)

75 cl bottle of good red wine (such as claret or merlot)
12 lumps of sugar
6 cloves
1 orange, sliced thinly
570 ml (1 pint) boiling water
150 ml (¼ pint) orange curaçao
150 ml (¼ pint) brandy
freshly grated nutmeg

Pour the wine into a large stainless steel saucepan. Add the sugar, cloves and orange slices, and heat until the liquid is coming to the boil. (Don't let it boil as that will destroy the alcohol.) Add the boiling water, orange curaçao and brandy, and stir well.

To serve, pour into a warmed punch bowl or cast-iron casserole dish. Ladle some of the mulled wine into each glass and top with a little freshly grated nutmeg.

HOT CHOCOLATE

Even if something as sinful as a cup of hot chocolate has to be off the menu for the rest of the year, it makes a delicious treat on a frosty December morning. And you can always burn off the calories with some dedicated Christmas shopping, which is often more than enough to make anyone break out in a sweat.

Serves 2 self-controlled people or 1 greedy-guts

570 ml (1 pint) whole or semi-skimmed milk
100 g (3½ oz) plain chocolate
sugar to taste
whipping cream if wished
ground cinnamon or cocoa powder

Break the chocolate into small pieces. Gently heat the milk until it is simmering, then take off the heat, drop in the chocolate pieces and stir well until all the chocolate has melted. Return to the heat and simmer for about 4 minutes, stirring all the time with a small whisk. In the meantime, warm the cups or mugs in readiness. Taste the hot chocolate and add a little sugar if you wish.

Pour the hot chocolate into the cups or mugs, top with a good dollop of whipped cream if you fancy going for broke, and sprinkle with a tiny amount of ground cinnamon or cocoa powder (or both).

DECK THE HALLS

The mistletoe hung in the castle hall,
The holly branch shone on the old oak wall.

'THE MISTLETOE BOUGH', THOMAS HAYNES BAYLY

O TANNENBAUM

Would Christmas be the same without a tree, swathed in fairy lights, decorated with baubles and with an ever-growing pile of gifts piled around its base? For most of us, it's hard to imagine its absence, even if it can take up half the room and it crashes to the floor every time the cat takes up residence in its branches.

Although the Christmas tree is a fixture of the festivities, it is a relatively recent arrival. Or is it? Well, yes and no.

❦ The earliest Christmas trees ❦

As with so many other elements of our modern Christmas, the tree is an echo of our pagan past. Long before Christianity reached the British Isles, our ancestors were celebrating trees at midwinter. They might not have hacked them down and borne them off to their homes simply to provide decoration, but they certainly revered them in the woods and forests where they grew. This would have been a way of honouring nature at the time of year when she appeared to have gone to sleep, and acted as a reminder that she would gradually come to life again now that the darkest time of the year was passing.

A story about St Boniface, who was born in Crediton in Devon in the seventh century, combines these pagan influences with Christianity. St Boniface was a missionary who was particularly active in what is now Germany and Bavaria. He was in Bavaria during the winter solstice when he was horrified to discover a group of people honouring an oak tree in a forest. Seizing an axe, St Boniface stopped what he regarded as this pagan blasphemy by chopping down the tree and praying to God. Apparently this did the trick and the pagans, who were obviously very good natured, were converted to Christianity on the spot. There are various accounts of what happened next. Some sources say that St Boniface planted a young fir tree in place of the oak, to symbolise God's everlasting love. Other sources claim that even as the oak tree crashed to the forest floor, a young fir tree sprang up in its place. In the ensuing years, the newly converted Christians would return to the forest to decorate the fir tree to mark Christmas. Eventually, it is said, this tradition spread in Bavaria and people began decorating their homes with fir trees. (The German folk song, 'O *Tannenbaum*', is in praise of the fir tree.)

∾ Starry night ∾

Another story concerns Martin Luther, the sixteenth-century Protestant reformer. One frosty winter's night in 1536, he was walking home through a forest in Wittenburg in Saxony. The sight of the stars twinkling through the trees inspired him to put candles on a fir tree in his own home, to symbolise the heavens.

∾ The Paradise tree ∾

A third theory about the origins of the Christmas tree is that it is a representation of the tree of Paradise from which Adam and Eve ate the forbidden fruit. In place of the fruit that tempted them, we hang glass baubles. An interesting footnote to this is that, although Adam and Eve are not official saints, their name day is 24 December in many Northern European countries.

∾ A German tradition ∾

Regardless of how the tradition started, craftsmen's guilds in Germany began to decorate their guild halls with trees in the four-teenth and fifteenth centuries. The trees were often adorned with fruits and nuts, which were picked off by children on Christmas Day. The custom eventually spread to the homes of those who could afford it, but was largely regarded as a Protestant tradition, with the

Roman Catholics preferring to decorate their homes with a Nativity scene.

❦ Christmas trees arrive in Britain ❦

It is often claimed that Prince Albert, the German-born consort of Queen Victoria, first introduced the Christmas tree to Britain. However, that is not true, and the accolade belongs to another German member of the British Royal Family.

When Charlotte, the daughter of the Duke of Mecklenburg-Strelitz, married King George III in 1761, it was only natural that she would want to continue some of her family traditions in her new home. One of these was to decorate the bough of a yew tree each Christmas with wax tapers and gifts. Members of the court gathered round the decoration, sang carols and received presents from Queen Charlotte. Everyone loved it.

On Christmas afternoon in 1800, Queen Charlotte threw a children's party at Queen's Lodge in Windsor. Rather than decorating a yew bough, she chose to pot up and decorate an entire yew tree. She adorned it with tiny wax candles, sweets, toys and raisins wrapped in paper. When the children arrived, they were enchanted. The adults were equally captivated.

Soon, anyone who was anyone couldn't raise their head in society unless they had a fully grown and lavishly decorated Christmas tree. My dear, anything else was unthinkable.

❦ One's royal tree ❦

The young Queen Victoria married Prince Albert of Saxe-Coburg and Gotha in 1840, and that Christmas he had several spruce trees sent over from Germany. In 1841, when she was the doting mother of two babies, Queen Victoria wrote in her diary:

> Today I have two children of my own to give presents to, who, they know not why, are full of happy wonder at the German Christmas tree and its radiant candles.

The public was thirsty for news of the young couple and their growing family, and several magazines and periodicals did their best to satisfy this national sense of curiosity. In 1848, the *Illustrated London News* published a woodcut of the young Royal Family gathered around their magnificent Christmas tree at Osborne House on the Isle of Wight. This is the image (with suitable amendments to make them look like an ordinary family) that crossed the Atlantic in 1850 and appeared in the very popular American magazine *Godey's Lady's Book*. For many readers, it was their first sight of a decorated Christmas tree, and now they wanted one too. Twenty years later, what had started as a fashionable trend had become an almost universal tradition.

❧ Christmas at 'the big house' ❧

Christmas trees continued to grow in popularity in Britain, too. The owners of grand country houses, with their legions of staff, would hold lavish Christmas house parties in Victorian and Edwardian times. It became the tradition for everyone above and below stairs to gather around the lighted Christmas tree on Christmas afternoon, and for gifts to be distributed to all the staff and their children, who would be wide-eyed with wonder at the massive tree a-glitter with shining baubles and lighted candles.

LIGHTING UP TIME

One of the great glories of Christmas trees is their lights. When they work, of course. There is nothing more irritating than getting last year's lights out of their box, unravelling the long wire and draping the lights around the tree so they are evenly distributed and not bunched up on one side, and then switching them on. Then finding that they aren't working, or they flicker on and off in a way that makes you worry it will all end in a big bang and singed eyebrows.

We have found ways of illuminating Christmas trees ever since we first hit on the brilliant idea of bringing a tree indoors and decorating it each December. Our ancestors decorated their trees with candles, which they originally pinned in place. Later, some clever manufacturers developed tiny candleholders that clipped on to the tree's branches. These were a fantastic idea until you tried to use them, because if the candle was too heavy it listed to one side, dripping hot wax on to the lower branches, the presents and, finally, the carpet. And there was always the exciting possibility of the candle flame setting light to the tree or melting the chocolate decorations.

Strings of electric lights for Christmas trees followed shortly after Joseph Swan patented the light bulb in Britain in 1880, a year after Thomas Edison had secured his own patent in the United States. At first, of course, electricity was an expensive luxury for the very few. Edward Hibberd Johnson, one of the lucky minority, decorated his New York Christmas tree with a string of eighty electric lights, in suitably patriotic red, white and blue, in December 1882. He happened to be the vice president of the Edison Electric Light Company, which may have had something to do with it.

The idea of electric Christmas lights was slow to catch on. Rather like the candles they replaced, it didn't help that they were relatively quick to catch fire. The bulbs could get very hot and, at that time, home wiring wasn't always completely reliable. It certainly wasn't recommended that you left the bulbs unattended.

For the first time, in December 1935, Selfridges, one of London's most famous department stores, was ablaze with light from the illuminated Christmas trees that stood between the columns ranged along its façade. Within a few years, the Second World War intervened with its nightly blackout, in which no one was allowed to show a light in case it attracted enemy bombers.

Money was scarce after the war and London's streets remained unadorned until 1954, when the businesses that made up the Regent Street Association clubbed together and paid for Regent Street to be decorated with strings of Christmas lights. This was such a welcome and cheery sight in post-war Britain that thousands of members of the public flocked to see them and questions were asked in the House of Lords about the resulting chaos. The Oxford Street Association followed Regent Street's lead in 1959 with its own Christmas lights.

Unfortunately it seems that recessions come round almost as frequently as Christmas, and in 1967 Oxford Street switched off its Christmas lights because of a lack of funds. Regent Street did the same in 1971, and neither resumed normal Christmas service until 1978. They have been going strong, albeit with mixed reviews, ever since.

LET'S PULL ANOTHER ONE!

They often promise more than they deliver, they frequently contain the most toe-curlingly obvious jokes, their trinkets can be mere fripperies and very few people look good in their paper hats, yet for many of us crackers are an essential part of Christmas.

A cracking good start

We have a young confectioner and baker called Tom Smith to thank for the Christmas cracker. During a business trip to Paris, he was inspired by the bonbons – sugared almonds wrapped in a twist of tissue paper – that were so popular there. He thought these would go down well in London, and he was right – the bonbons he sold in his shop during the Christmas of 1847 were a roaring success. But he soon realised that their sales were completely seasonal. How could he make his bonbons more attractive and increase their saleability?

The developments continue

Over time, Tom Smith came up with two brilliant ideas. First, he put a love motto into each bonbon, and some time later he added a strip of paper that made a satisfying crack when it was pulled in half. Then, he made the bonbons bigger, so they could be pulled more easily. They were a huge success, but there was still room for improvement. The love motto stayed but out went the sugared almond, to be replaced with a small gift. Out went the name 'bonbons', as well, to be replaced with 'Cosaques', which was much more exotic. This name alluded to the bang that the crackers made when they were pulled: at the time, firecrackers were often called 'cossacks' because they sounded like the crack of a cossack's whip.

The crackers continued to evolve. They had to, because rival companies were now competing for the lucrative Christmas market. The love motto fell out of favour, and the mottoes first became topical and eventually turned into rhymes, riddles and jokes. The hats, made from the best tissue paper, and then balloons were added to what were now called 'crackers'.

Today, you can buy crackers to suit every purse, from the cheapest box of supermarket crackers to fabulously expensive offerings containing suitably lavish gifts.

⬱ Clever tactics ⬱

We all have different ways of pulling crackers, although by necessity this always involves at least two people. Sometimes, in a large group, everyone prefers to cross their arms and pull the crackers in unison, which often results in the hats and gifts flying around the room or landing in the brandy butter. Alternatively, everyone may have to take turns.

One unwritten rule is that the person left holding the bulk of the cracker is allowed to keep its contents. There is a secret to this which works in the majority of cases: when the time comes to pull the cracker, don't do it. Let the other person do all the pulling. All they'll get for their effort is the small end of the cracker. They may also fall off their chair, so be ready with plenty of sympathy. After you've put on your paper hat, of course.

DECORATIVE DELIGHTS

Many of our Christmas decorations are so familiar to us that we tend to take them for granted and never stop to think about how or why they originated. Here are some of the things that are synonymous with a traditional Christmas.

❧ Baubles ❧

For those of us who adore a good session of nostalgia, one of the great pleasures of Christmas is to unpack the baubles that go on the Christmas tree and to remember where they all came from. And if they're made from glass, and therefore quite precious and delicate, so much the better.

Glass baubles originated in 1847 in a glassworks run by the Greiner family in Lauscha, a small town in Germany. The glass was hand-blown into clay moulds and finished off with a special silvering technique, and the resulting decorations soon became very popular at Christmas. It wasn't long before they were being exported, and they first arrived in Britain in the 1870s.

❧ On top of the tree ❧

Why do we put an angel on top of our Christmas trees? Because the Angel Gabriel told the Virgin Mary that she was going to bear a son, and because angels also appear elsewhere in the story of the Nativity. Generations of small children have made Christmas tree angels from cones of stiff white paper, and given them cut-out wings and cotton wool for hair.

Alternatively, we might put a star on the top of the tree. This is, of course, to symbolise the star that guided the Magi to the stable in which the baby Jesus lay.

❧ Tinsel ❧

Tinsel has so many uses. You can swathe the Christmas tree in it until you can barely see any branches, bind it around the banisters, drape it across the mantelpiece, wear it as a hairband if you're feeling brave and even make a simple Christmassy badge by twining a short length of it around a small safety pin.

Today's tinsel is glittery, available in lots of different colours and is usually made from PVC. But when it was first developed in Germany in the seventeenth century, it looked very different. In those days, it consisted of long narrow strips of silver, which glittered beautifully in firelight and candlelight. Unfortunately, silver is expensive and it soon tarnishes, so alternative metals were used, including lead and aluminium. All of these draped beautifully, thanks to their weight.

❧ Yum yum ❧

Christmas is one of the big Christian feasts, so it is hardly surprising that most well-dressed Christmas trees are hung with something to eat. In Germany, the first Christmas trees were decorated with almonds, fruit and other goodies. When the fashion for Christmas trees arrived in Britain, they were often adorned with fruits, sweets, sugared almonds wrapped in twists of paper or even little paper cornucopias filled with edible goodies. Gingerbread biscuits, strung with ribbon, became popular too, and eventually the chocolate manufacturers hit on the bright idea of producing special tree decorations, moulded into festive shapes such as Father Christmases, bells and parcels, and wrapped in shiny coloured foil. These have been going strong for decades, but it's remarkable how quickly they apparently vanish from the tree even though no one admits to having eaten them.

ADVENT WREATHS

One of the traditional ways of marking the four Sundays of Advent is with a special evergreen ring known as an Advent wreath. The jury is out as to whether this is a throwback to an age-old pagan custom or whether it originated in Germany in the sixteenth or nineteenth centuries. Perhaps its origins don't matter. But its significance certainly does.

The Advent wreath is decorated with four, or possibly five, candles. On the first Sunday in Advent, only the first candle is lit. On the second Sunday, the first and second candles are lit, and so on until the fourth Sunday in Advent, when all four candles are lit. If there is a fifth candle in the centre of the wreath, it is lit on Christmas Day.

Each candle has a particular significance within some parts of the Christian Church. The first candle is a reminder of the hope that Jesus Christ brings, and it is lit in honour of the patriarchs of the Church. The second candle is the candle of the peace, and is lit in remembrance of the prophets who foretold the coming of Christ. The third candle is the candle of love, and is lit to honour John the Baptist, who was Christ's cousin. The fourth candle is the candle of joy, and is lit in remembrance of Mary, the mother of Christ. The fifth candle, which is lit in churches on Christmas Day, puts Christ himself at the very heart of the Christmas season.

KISS KISS

Fashions come and fashions go but mistletoe has been an essential element of a happy Christmas for centuries. This must surely have something to do with the tradition of kissing beneath it, so generous bunches of it were suspended from every possible surface, including ceilings and doorways. The bunches had to be generous because every time a kiss was claimed, you were supposed to pick off a berry.

～ The kissing bough ～

Before Christmas trees became a ubiquitous decoration in most British homes, people used to hang balls of greenery from their ceilings. These were called kissing boughs, and they were made from branches of evergreens, such as holly, rosemary and ivy, that were wrapped around two hoops to form an open sphere. Some people liked to suspend red apples in the middle of the sphere, while others preferred to hang up wooden figures of Mary, Joseph and the infant Jesus. A few candles were fixed to the kissing bough as well, and then a bunch of mistletoe was attached to the base of the bough before it was hung in position on Christmas Eve.

The mistletoe was an important part of the kissing bough because of the tradition about kissing under the mistletoe. Whenever a man got his kiss, he would pull off one of the mistletoe berries. This meant, of course, that it was essential to get the kissing bough at the right height, because if it was too low it got in everyone's way, and if it was too high no one could get at the mistletoe. When all the berries had gone, no one could kiss beneath the bough any longer.

❧ Unkissed and unmarried ❧

It was essential for every unmarried girl to be kissed at least once beneath the mistletoe each Christmas. If she didn't achieve this, tradition told her that she could write off any chance of marching up the aisle in the coming year. However, sleeping with a sprig of mistletoe tucked beneath her pillow was said to make her dream of her future husband – even if she wouldn't be marrying him any time soon.

SO FIR, SO GOOD

Do you like your Christmas trees real or artificial? Choosing an artificial tree can be a complicated business – do you select one that makes a virtue of being fake by having branches that change colour in a constant light show, or do you go for one that's as similar to the real thing as you can find? Decisions, decisions!

If you opt for a real tree, you might imagine that there are fewer decisions to make. After all, one fir tree is much like another, you might reason, and for many people the most important considerations are the size and width of the thing. It will be a bore if the only way to get into the sitting room over Christmas is to sidle in while sucking in your tummy. This, in itself, is often an impossible feat during the festive season, and it also means there's no chance of watching an old film while happily chomping your way through a plate of leftovers.

The fact is, though, that one fir tree isn't much like another. There is quite a lot to consider when choosing the right Christmas tree.

Blue spruce (*Picea pungens*)

As its common name suggests, this tree's needles have a slightly bluish hue. It is a very attractive tree but is not always easy to track down.

Fraser fir (*Abies fraseri*)

This is perfect if space is limited because the trees are narrow and compact. The branches are strong and the citrus-scented needles fairly soft, making it a good choice if you enjoy lavishly decorating your Christmas tree. What is more, it holds on to its needles for a long time.

Noble fir (*Abies procera*)

Noble by name, noble by nature – this is often called 'the king of Christmas trees'. It holds its aromatic, glaucous blue-green needles well, and the lower branches can be snapped off at the trunk and used for wreaths and other decorations.

Nordmann fir (*Abies nordmanniana*)

They say you get what you pay for, so while this tree is expensive it is also attractive and long-lasting, with a bushy shape, fat branches and soft, glossy needles.

Norway spruce (*Abies picea*)

Whether you choose a cut tree or one that is container-grown, you must water the Norway spruce lavishly otherwise it will shed its needles remorselessly and you'll still be finding them in the summer. It has light green needles, a neat triangular shape and that classic Christmas tree scent.

≈ Scots pine (*Pinus sylvestris*) ≈

This tree is native to the UK and has a strong pine fragrance. Its blue-green needles are soft and long. It has a more open centre than many other Christmas trees.

≈ Serbian spruce (*Picea omorika*) ≈

One of the bonuses of the Serbian spruce is that it often bears small cones when bought as a Christmas tree, because it flowers early. Its branches point slightly upwards, so decorations are less likely to slip off, but it is prone to shedding its needles.

THE REAL DEAL

If you've decided to share your Christmas with a real Christmas tree, whether it's container grown or has been severed from its roots, it makes sense to take care of it so it continues to look its best right through until Twelfth Night.

❧ Container-grown trees ❧

If you are opting for one of these trees, make sure it has spent its life in its container and hasn't recently been dug up and put in its pot (such trees are usually described as 'containerised' or 'potted'), as this can result in badly damaged roots.

When you're buying the tree, choose one that looks healthy and isn't pot-bound (where the tree has grown too big for its pot, with lots of roots growing through the holes in the bottom). Give it a good drink of fresh water when you get it home, and leave it outdoors in a cool shed or garage until you are ready to decorate it.

The one disadvantage of a container-grown tree is that it won't enjoy being in a centrally heated room. You might like to spend your Christmas feeling warm and cosy, but your tree won't. Unfortunately, that means you should bring the tree indoors as close to Christmas Day as possible, to prevent it looking sad and tatty by Twelfth Night.

When you do bring the tree indoors, you should keep it away from open fires, radiators and direct sunlight because these will quickly dehydrate the tree. Ideally, it should be placed in a cool room. Place the container on a large waterproof saucer, because you will have to water the tree every day to keep it looking good. If it really starts to suffer, you will have to remove its lights and decorations and put it outside to recover.

The great advantage of a container-grown tree is that you can keep it outside throughout the year, potting it on to a bigger pot with plenty of fresh compost, and bring it indoors again the following Christmas.

At some point, the tree will get so big that you'll struggle to carry it indoors. This is the time to give it a happy retirement by planting it in the garden, but do bear in mind that it will romp away once its roots get established and it will take up a lot of space.

❧ Cut trees ❧

The best way to care for a Christmas tree that has had its roots cut off is to treat it like a gigantic cut flower. Essentially, this means it needs three things: water, water and water. Ideally, you should have a special stand that will support the trunk while keeping the cut end immersed in water. Putting the trunk in a pot of sand or soil may seem like a good idea but it will restrict the tree's ability to take up water, and therefore will reduce its life expectancy and increase the chances of it becoming a very sorry specimen by Twelfth Night (and also the likelihood of your living room floor becoming overrun by needles).

When you've got the tree home, stand the trunk in a bucket of clean cold water and leave it in an outside shed or in the garage. As with a container-grown tree, ideally you should bring the tree indoors as near to Christmas as possible.

When it's time to bring the tree inside, saw off the bottom couple of inches with a pruning saw, to increase its ability to take up water. Bring it inside and assemble it on its stand in a cool place, well away from any source of heat. Fill the inside of the stand with water, and remember to top it up daily to keep the tree alive.

OUT IN THE FRESH AIR

Frost performs its secret ministry,
Unhelped by any wind.

'FROST AT MIDNIGHT', SAMUEL TAYLOR COLERIDGE

PLANTING FOR BIRDS

L ate autumn, winter and early spring can be a tough time for birds. We can all help them by planting shrubs and trees that bear fruits and seeds at this time of year. Not only are these plants decorative but they provide food and shelter for many other creatures too.

Blackthorn (*Prunus spinosa*)

This is a fearsome plant with long spines, making it ideal for protective hedging. In the autumn it bears black fruits, known as sloes. You can use these to make sloe gin, but leave plenty on the shrub for the birds who like them too.

Cotoneaster spp.

You will find many varieties of cotoneaster, from those that grow up walls to those that lie prostrate on the ground. They bear masses of small orange berries in the autumn, and tiny flowers in the spring which provide an important food for bees.

Crab apple (*Malus sylvestris*)

We have been growing crab apples in our gardens for centuries, and livened up our Christmas festivities with the help of roasted crab apples hissing in bowls of wassail. These small trees bear clusters of orange fruits in the autumn, much to the delight of birds including starlings, robins, greenfinches and thrushes.

❧ Firethorn (*Pyracantha* spp.) ❧

This spiny shrub is loved by some and loathed by others, but it's a firm favourite with birds in the winter. Depending on the variety, the berries may be yellow, orange or scarlet.

❧ Guelder rose (*Viburnum opulus*) ❧

This is one of the most valuable shrubs in the garden because it bears beautiful purple berries in the autumn and early winter, and creamy-white flowerheads in the summer. Birds love the berries, which are particular favourites of mistle thrushes and bullfinches.

❧ Hawthorn (*Crataegus monogyna*) ❧

This thorny shrub has been used as hedging, especially around fields, for hundreds of years. Many creatures benefit from it throughout the year, and in the autumn the berries (known as 'haws') are a valuable food for many birds, including blackbirds, greenfinches, thrushes, yellowhammers and chaffinches.

❧ Holly (*Ilex* spp.) ❧

Holly trees are either male or female, and a female plant can only bear berries if it is pollinated by a nearby male plant. Depending on the variety of holly, the berries can be yellow, orange or scarlet. Many birds eat the berries, including fieldfares, thrushes, redwings and blackbirds.

✍ Honeysuckle (*Lonicera periclymenum*) ✍

After bearing sweetly scented and highly decorative flowers in the summer, honeysuckle produces masses of berries in the autumn. These are particularly attractive to warblers, bullfinches and thrushes.

✍ Ivy (*Hedera helix*) ✍

Ivy may be the enemy of brickwork, because of its habit of insinuating its tenacious roots into the mortar and gradually penetrating walls, but its berries make it the friend of birds in the winter. Ivy berries turn from green to black in December, by which time many of the autumn-fruiting plants have been stripped bare, and are a particular favourite of blackbirds and thrushes.

✍ Rose (*Rosa* spp.) ✍

There are thousands of different varieties of rose, from tiny patio roses to sprawling climbers that will cover even the biggest garden shed in seemingly no time at all. But if you are choosing roses with wildlife in mind, it is best to plant those that bear single flowers, so the stamens are easily accessible to bees and other nectar-eating insects. If you leave the dead roses on the plant they will turn into beautiful rosehips in late autumn, much loved by birds.

SNOW BUSINESS

Traditional Christmas card scenes often show stagecoaches dashing across a landscape white with snow, or a perky robin perched on a snow-covered gate with a sprig of greenery held jauntily in its beak. Some of the most memorable Christmas films involve at least one snowfall, and even crime novels set at Christmas frequently feature plenty of snow. Because it seems that, for many of us, Christmas simply isn't Christmas without some gently falling white stuff. At which point, of course, it is described as a white Christmas. But what exactly does that mean?

In the UK, the precise definition of a white Christmas is that at least one flake of snow has fallen in a specified spot (frequently the roof of the Met Office) at some point between midnight on Christmas Eve and midnight on Christmas Day.

Unfortunately, the British weather doesn't always oblige and Christmas Day is often unseasonably mild and damp. Has it been like that for centuries? Apparently not. We went through what has become known as the Little Ice Age between the sixteenth and nineteenth centuries. This was a period of consistently lower temperatures in Britain, bringing some bitterly cold winters. The River Thames sometimes froze over so thickly in London (partly because its flow was dramatically slowed up by the old London Bridge) that it was safe to hold frost fairs on the compacted ice. These fairs attracted everyone, from young children to members of the Royal Family. Charles II attended a frost fair during the terrible winter of 1683–4 and, in common with many of his subjects, bought a special certificate to prove he'd been there. The Thames was nothing but thick ice for two months, while the ground in Somerset was apparently frozen to a depth of four feet. It sounds picturesque, but it is hard to imagine the suffering this must have caused in a world without our modern comforts of double glazing, central heating and hot water on tap.

Speaking of hot water, it didn't figure in the Reverend Francis Kilvert's bath on Christmas morning, 1870. He had woken to a severe frost. He recorded the experience in his diary:

> I sat down in my bath upon a sheet of thick ice which broke in the middle into large pieces whilst sharp points and jagged edges stuck all round the sides of the tub like *chevaux de frise*, not particularly comforting to the naked thighs and loins, for the keen ice cut like broken glass.

Even his bath sponge had turned to a ball of ice and had to be thawed out between his palms before he could use it. Luckily, the icy water made his skin burn, which must have given some semblance of warmth before the convulsive shivering set in.

BUILDING A SNOWMAN

In an ideal world, Christmas coincides with a thick fall of snow. Your friends and family have all arrived to stay, so you don't have to worry about them being in peril on icy roads. You've had the foresight to lay in plenty of food, so there are no concerns about trekking to the shops because you've run out of milk, and log fires are burning merrily in every grate. You've just had a hearty lunch and now you need to work off all that food in readiness for an equally hearty slice of Christmas cake at teatime, followed by a really good supper that will help you to stave off any dangers of night starvation. So, what to do? The answer is obvious. Wrap up warm and go outside to build a snowman.

❧ Choose the right clothes ❧

The wrapping up warm bit of that instruction is particularly important. A shivering fit will spoil your fun, as will the realisation that you can no longer feel your fingers or toes. It pays to choose the right gloves, too, as it is a nuisance when woollen gloves, normally so cosy, turn sopping wet, freezing cold and are prettily decorated with baubles of snow and ice that eventually stop you doing anything. We are going for substance over style here, so consider wearing a pair of woollen gloves next to your skin and a pair of rubber gloves over the top of them (but do check the gloves for holes, for obvious reasons).

❧ Choose the right location ❧

It pays to put some thought into this. You want it to be somewhere that has plenty of snow, because it will be hard work to carry it over from somewhere else. You must also make sure – as far as possible, considering that everything will be blanketed in snow – that the area of ground you've chosen doesn't contain any potential obstacles, such as bricks, pots or steps, that could easily send you flying. You want your Christmas to be white in terms of snow, not plaster casts.

It will also endear you to other members of the household if you don't decide to build your snowman in the middle of a frequently used path or slap bang in front of someone's car.

✺ Making a snowball ✺

Now comes the fun part. Grab a big blob of snow and pack it tightly together between your hands until you can hear it making a crunching noise, as though making a very hard snowball. Failure to do this will make it difficult to move on to the next stage because everything is likely to fall apart, and instead of creating a snowman you'll have a brief snow shower.

✺ Let it roll ✺

Grab another handful of snow and pack it round your snowball to make it hard. And another. And another, until you'd knock someone out with your snowball if you were to throw it at them. Resist the temptation to try this so you can see what happens.

Now start to roll the tightly packed snowball through the snow. It will get fatter as it rolls along. Every now and then, stop to pat the snow into place. Continue this process until the snowball is big enough to form the lower half of the snowman's body. The exact size is up to you, and is also determined by the amount of snow at your disposal. Steer the large snowball into position and gently pat its outline to compress the snow. Be careful when doing this if the snow is powdery, in case the snowball shatters. If possible, dig out a little snow on the top of the ball, in readiness for the next step.

✺ Getting a-head ✺

It is now time to make the snowman's head. You do this in the same way that you made his body, while remembering that his head will be smaller. When it seems to be the right size, pat it firmly with your hands, then lift it on to the snowman's body. This is where the indentation on top of his body comes in, because it will make it easier to attach his head to his body without it falling off. Pack some loose snow around the point where his head meets his body, to strengthen the join.

⇜ The main features ⇝

You could leave your snowman like this, but you won't know which way he's looking unless you give him a face. The classic choice for this is two lumps of coal for his eyes and a carrot for his nose, plus a pipe to shove in his non-existent mouth. You can keep him warm by giving him an old scarf and a hat, and if you wish you can give him buttons down his front using more pieces of coal.

⇜ The snow family ⇝

If time, snow and your circulation allow, you can make an entire family of big and little snowmen. Or snowpeople, for those of a politically correct disposition.

WHEE!

Whenever there is a decent snowfall, many of us are gripped by an urgent desire to head for the hills. Once there, we get out our sledge or toboggan, tramp to the top of the most suitable hill and whiz all the way down it. Then, when we reach the bottom – still in one piece, with luck – we climb back up to the top of the hill and do it all over again. And again.

❧ Do it yourself ❧

Unless you have planned in advance and bought a sledge during mild weather, when no one else has had the same brilliant idea, the moment the snow starts falling you won't be able to buy one at all because everyone will have beaten you to it. Or, if the weather is really bad, the snow will have stopped deliveries of sledges getting through. Oh, the irony.

The answer is to make your own. If you are small and light you can use an old plastic tray. You can also make a decent impromptu sledge by stuffing a sturdy plastic sack (such as one that once held potting compost or coal) with an old cushion, tying up the opening with some thick string and holding on to this end as you rush down the hill. Before each run, make sure the string is securely fastened, otherwise you will soon part company with the sledge and its innards. If you can't find a suitable cushion, a bundle of old clothes or towels will do just as well. With this method the bigger you are the faster you go!

❧ Safety first ❧

Whatever you decide to use as a last-minute sledge, it is of course essential for it to be safe – not only for you but also for anyone who might accidentally come into contact with it. Sledging is great fun but it also has the potential to be highly dangerous. Avoid using anything metal with sharp corners, and always behave responsibly. It is also wise to keep away from areas with lots of trees, to avoid the risk of cannoning into one of them at top speed. A trip to hospital is not the best way to round off a day's sledging.

CHRISTMAS GREENERY

Sometimes tradition and beauty go hand in hand, and that is certainly true when it comes to Christmas decorations. We have been cutting evergreen plants and decorating our homes with them for centuries. Once, we would have cut them from woods, forests and gardens. Today, we can buy them from nurseries, florists' and greengrocers' shops, but it is also good to grow these plants in our own gardens. Here are some of the most seasonal and decorative plants. Some of them have the added attraction of being considered magical or otherwise special in some way.

Given the vagaries of British autumns and winters, sometimes these plants will be in their prime at Christmas and at other times they may already be looking tatty and past their best. It depends entirely on the weather, which is why it's a good idea to grow a wide variety of plants, so there is always something to pick.

❧ Alder catkins (*Alnus glutinosa*) ❧

Alder is a common tree for moist conditions, and frequently grows on the banks of rivers and marshes. Its catkins are not particularly decorative on their own, but they add interest to vases of greenery. The long catkins are male and are always borne next to the small female flowers that look like tiny cones.

❧ Bay (*Laurus nobilis*) ❧

This evergreen shrub can grow into a sizable tree if left unpruned. Its fragrant leaves can be dried and used sparingly in sauces, soups and casseroles, but they are also highly ornamental at Christmastime. You can use the cut branches or tear up individual leaves and put them in home-made pot pourri.

❧ Box (*Buxus sempervirens*) ❧

Box has tiny mid-green leaves that look good in small decorations. However, the leaves are prone to being blasted by cold winds, so they must be chosen carefully, otherwise they will look ragged when you get them indoors.

❧ Hazel catkins (*Corylus avellana*) ❧

Hazel was once one of the most important trees in Britain because it was so widely grown for coppicing, which meant it provided firewood as well as long poles for use in building. A hazel tree can live for hundreds of years and has always been deemed to have magical properties.

Its flowers appear as long pale green catkins that are an interesting addition to Christmas greenery, provided that they are produced in time. This depends entirely on whether it is a mild or a cold winter.

❧ Holly (*Ilex aquifolium*) ❧

There are many species of holly, but *Ilex aquifolium* is native to Britain. This particular species is dioecious, which means that each plant is single-sex and will bear flowers that are only of that sex. If you want berries, which after all are almost essential Christmas decorations, you must plant both a male and a female tree.

We stick a sprig of holly (whether real or plastic) on our Christmas puddings, but there are many other ways to decorate our homes with holly. A big vase of nothing but this glossy, spiny shrub can look terrific, especially if it bears bright red berries. In addition to the typical dark green variety of holly, there are variegated varieties, plus those without spines. Sprigs of green holly look good in outdoor wreaths and withstand even the worst weather.

∼ Ivy (*Hedera helix*) ∼

This is one of the most versatile plants of all for Christmas decorations. If you are growing it yourself, you will soon discover that you must be patient if you want to use ivy berries at Christmas. Juvenile ivy has typically ivy-shaped leaves but doesn't bear any flowers or berries; this only happens when the plant is adult, at which point its leaves have become diamond-shaped.

You can cut long trailing pieces for draping across picture frames and mirrors, over mantelpieces or for twining around banisters. You could even curl a very long piece of ivy into a small circle, securing it discreetly at several points, to make an informal wreath. The berries are green when immature and black when ripe, and they look marvellous in many different decorations. Do save some for the birds, though, who rely on them in the middle of winter because, unusually for berries, they are packed with protein instead of the more normal sugar.

∼ Laurustinus (*Viburnum tinus*) ∼

There are hundreds of varieties of viburnum but this one has glossy oval green leaves and bears fragrant pinky-white flowers. It looks particularly good in vases with other evergreens, but also in smaller decorations so its pretty flowers can be enjoyed in more detail.

∼ Rosemary (*Rosmarinus officinalis*) ∼

We have planted rosemary bushes in our gardens for centuries, not only because of their usefulness in cooking and keeping insects at bay, but also because they have always been thought to be an effective charm against witchcraft.

Rosemary was a popular Christmas decoration in the seventeenth century, no doubt because of the spicy scent of its needles as well as its overall appearance. Sprigs of rosemary provide a good contrast with plants that have rounded or oval leaves, and individual needles are a classic addition to pot pourri.

❧ Spotted laurel (*Aucuba japonica*) ❧

To some, this is a much-loved shrub, while for others it is a horticultural horror. But its glossy, white-speckled leaves and scarlet berries make it a valuable Christmas decoration, especially in winters when other suitable plants are looking weather-beaten.

❧ Yew (*Taxus baccata*) ❧

If you are of a nervous disposition, you might not want to include yew in your Christmas decorations because it is a plant traditionally associated with death and churchyards. But if you can overcome your prejudice you will find that small sprigs of yew look lovely when tied with scarlet ribbon and left on windowsills or mantelpieces. Keep it away from inquisitive children, because every part of it is poisonous.

ROBIN REDBREAST

Of all the British birds in our gardens, the robin (*Erithacus rubecula*) is the one most closely associated with Christmas. It regularly appears on Christmas cards, often surrounded by snow, which forms a delightful contrast with its red breast and bright black eyes. But why are robins so strongly connected with Christmas when there are so many other native birds to choose from?

☙ Robins and the Nativity ❧

One story says that it was getting chilly in the stable after Jesus was born because the fire that had been lit to keep the Holy Family warm was going out. Mary asked all the animals that had gathered there if they could help to keep the fire going but none of them volunteered. Finally, a small, nondescript brown robin flew over to the fire and fluttered there, fanning the embers with its wings until the flames leapt up again. Then it flew off and returned with twigs in its beak to put on the fire. A spark jumped out of the fire and caught the bird on the chest, turning it red. Apparently Mary was so grateful to the little bird for its efforts in keeping her baby warm that she declared it would always have a red breast as a symbol of its kind heart.

☙ Robins and the Crucifixion ❧

In addition to being associated with the beginning of Jesus's life, robins have a traditional connection with the end of it as well. Legend has it that when Christ was dying in agony on the cross, a brown robin landed on his head and tried to pull off his crown of thorns to relieve the pain. Some of Jesus's blood splashed on to the bird's breast, forever staining it red as a reminder of its considerate nature.

Delightful though this story is, it is somewhat ironic, since the robin has the reputation of being a most aggressive and territorial bird, allegedly fighting its fellow robins to the death if necessary. Perhaps that is why there is another legend connected with the robin's red breast: the robin once used to carry water to sinners who were burning in hell, and the flames singed its breast.

≈ Robins and redbreasts ≈

It is often claimed that postmen were called 'redbreasts' because they were seen dashing about with the Christmas mail in their red waist-coats, but this is a popular myth. The first Royal Mail uniforms, which were issued for mail coach guards in 1784, consisted of scarlet coats with blue lapels. Scarlet continued to be an important element of the uniforms although there were no red waistcoats. These belonged to the Bow Street Runners, the precursors of the British professional police force, who wore red waistcoats that earned them the nickname 'redbreasts'. Charles Dickens wrote, in a letter, that 'the Bow Street Runners ... had no other uniform than a blue dress-coat, brass buttons ... and a bright red cloth waistcoat. The waistcoat was indispensable, and the slang name for them was "red-breasts", in consequence.'

Regardless of who wore the waistcoats, when it became fashion-able to send Christmas cards from the 1840s onwards, robins soon became associated with the Christmas post and have remained so ever since.

THE MYSTERY OF MISTLETOE

If you want to keep witches and goblins at bay, what you need is some mistletoe. Apparently, these mischievous creatures don't like it one bit. According to tradition, it's a wonderfully handy plant to have around for all sorts of other reasons too. But you've got to find it first, because it doesn't grow everywhere. It's a parasite, growing on host trees, and it will happily flourish on some while spurning others of the same variety. It also favours some parts of the country over others, so this is definitely something to investigate for those who fancy becoming mistletoe farmers.

There are several varieties growing in different parts of the world. *Viscum album* is the European mistletoe and is native to Great

Britain and other European countries, while *Phoradendron serotinum* is native to North America. As the *album* part of its botanical name suggests, European mistletoe bears white berries, but North American mistletoe berries can be white, yellow, orange or red.

European mistletoe grows on more than two hundred different trees, including apples, poplars and hawthorns. It is a hemiparasite: its upper body is a normal plant that produces leaves, flowers and berries, but its lower body consists of a shallow root, called a haustorium, that invades the host tree. The mistletoe berries are gelatinous and contain seeds. Birds love to eat these berries which are sticky, so the birds wipe their beaks on the branches of other trees and, in doing so, help to disperse the seeds. The seeds are also spread when birds excrete them. As you might imagine from its name, the mistle thrush (*Turdus viscivorus*) is particularly fond of mistletoe.

Many keen gardeners also do their best to get a crop of mistletoe by smearing seeds on to the branches of suitable trees. Unfortunately, the seeds often refuse to cooperate and fail to take, because it seems that they only grow where they want to, as opposed to where the gardener would like them to flourish.

❧ Mistletoe and mythology ❧

There is plenty of mythology surrounding mistletoe. In Norse mythology, mistletoe is connected with the death of Baldr, whose mother was Frigg and whose father, some say, was Odin. After Baldr had a series of troubling dreams that suggested he was going to die, Frigg exacted a promise from everything on earth that it wouldn't harm Baldr. But she omitted to ask mistletoe to keep the promise. Loki, who was a mischievous trickster god, found out about this and killed Baldr with a weapon made from mistletoe wood. One version of this story says that, after Baldr's death, mistletoe became associated with love, rather than the hatred that had motivated Loki's action.

Interestingly, some legends claim that Christ's cross was made from a variety of mistletoe wood. However, there are many other candidates for the source of the cross, most notably the elder (*Sambucus nigra*) tree.

According to the Latin historian Pliny, ancient Druids believed that mistletoe mustn't touch the ground once it's been cut, so they would lay a white cloak on the ground to catch it as it fell. Pliny wrote that Druids particularly valued mistletoe that grew on oak trees, especially if they cut it at a new moon using an implement that wasn't made from iron. They were reputed to use golden sickles for this important task.

Of course, we can't ignore mistletoe's associations with fertility, although extracting these from the tangle of conflicting legends that surrounds the plant isn't easy. The coda to the story of Baldr's death is one explanation, but another is surely the shape of the plant's leaves and central berry, and also the milky white fluid within the berries. Herbalists have long associated the shape of a plant with any part of the human body that resembles it (a rule called the doctrine of signatures), often with remarkably effective results.

THE HOLLY AND THE IVY

Several plants are associated with Christmas, but holly and ivy come top of most people's lists. These two plants look fantastic in Christmas decorations, they appear on Christmas cards and they are mentioned in several Christmas carols. What is more, a host of interesting stories and customs is associated with each of them, including the fact that holly was once considered to be a male plant and ivy was its female partner. There was also the element of good and bad about them, with holly being the 'good' plant and ivy the 'bad', no doubt owing at least in part to its associations with Druids.

∽ Holly ∽

The holly family (*Ilex* spp.) is huge. The British native holly (*Ilex aquifolium*) has tremendous religious significance at Christmas. Its prickly leaves are evocative of the crown of thorns that was placed on Jesus Christ's head at his crucifixion, and its scarlet berries are synonymous with drops of his blood. Yet, as with so many other things that are now associated with a traditional Christmas, holly was an important element of the midwinter celebrations long before the arrival of Christianity in Britain.

Red has long been believed to act as a charm against evil, so the holly's scarlet berries and its spiny leaves were the ideal antidote to mischief and malevolence at a time of year when so many protective plants are dormant. Our pagan Roman ancestors associated holly with their god Saturn. They would give one another sprigs of holly during Saturnalia, which was held in December, as a way of marking their friendship. They would also decorate their homes, both inside and out, with holly during Saturnalia.

Druids are also said to have valued the holly's berries so much that they would decorate their hair with holly. They believed that the berries represented the blood of their goddess.

As a result of these strong associations of midwinter with holly, it is hardly surprising that the plant became an important symbol of the Christmas celebrations. But it retained its magical qualities. John Parkinson, the seventeenth-century botanist, wrote about this combination of the sacred and the superstitious in his *Theatrum Botanicum*.

The branches with berries, are used at Christ tide to decke our houses withall, but that they should defend the house from lightning, and keep themselves from witchcraft, is a superstition of the Gentiles, learned from Pliny, saith Matthiolus.

Holly is mentioned in several Christmas carols, but perhaps the one that is best known is the traditional carol, 'The Holly and the Ivy', which tells us that 'of all the trees that are in the wood, the holly bears the crown'. As the carol continues, it associates the holly's lily white flowers with Christ's birth, and its berries 'as red as any blood' and prickles 'as sharp as any thorn' with his death.

There is another reason why holly is such a valued plant. Even though its prickles are sharp and off-putting to humans, apparently cattle have no such problems and actually enjoy eating the leaves. Holly was frequently used as winter fodder for cattle in medieval times. Perhaps that is why a sprig of Christmas holly was often left in a cattle shed in the hope that this would improve the animals' health.

∾ Ivy ∾

As with holly, there are several species of ivy (*Hedera* spp.), and the British native ivy is called *Hedera helix*. Perhaps because of its evergreen nature and its ability to withstand even the bitterest winter weather, it has also long been considered to have magical properties. In northern Scotland it was once hung in cattle sheds to keep evil spirits at bay and to protect the cows' milk. If you had whooping cough, it was believed that you would cure it by drinking out of a cup made from ivy wood.

Most memorably, ivy was twinned with holly in Christmas carols, often with some form of rivalry between them. Invariably, ivy seemed to come out the loser.

MAKING DO

Who with a little cannot be content,
Endures an everlasting punishment.

'AGAIN', ROBERT HERRICK

Our revels now are ended

Many of our children have grown up believing that it was the Grinch who stole Christmas, but he certainly wasn't the first to have a go at stamping out this most festive time of the year. In the sixteenth and seventeenth centuries, Christmas was a casualty of the Reformation, when Britain switched from being a Roman Catholic country to a Protestant one.

∾ The first attack on Christmas ∾

Christmas was first put under siege in Scotland, which turned its back on its Catholic roots in 1560 and created the Church of Scotland (popularly known as 'the Kirk'). Its founder was the Calvinist John Knox, who published the rather chilly-sounding *First Book of Discipline* in 1560. One of its edicts proclaimed that Christmas and other religious feast days had been invented by 'the Papists': they weren't mentioned in the Bible and therefore had nothing to do with scripture. The Virgin Mary and the saints were also deemed unscriptural. Even the name of the festival was an indication that it should be shunned, as Christmas means 'Christ's Mass', and the Reformation wanted nothing to do with masses. Another thorn in the side of the Kirk was the way in which people celebrated Christmas. They were having far too much fun.

The English writer Philip Stubbs didn't mince his words in his book *Anatomie of the Abuses in England*, in 1583:

> Who is ignorant that more mischief is that time committed than in all the years besides? ... Whereby robbery, whoredom, murder and what not is committed! What dicing and carding, what eating and drinking, what banqueting and feasting is then used! ... to the great dishonour of God and the impoverishing of the realm.

Such strong sentiments slowly gathered pace. By the 1570s the Scots were being punished for celebrating Christmas and singing 'filthy carols'. And so it continued, with the Kirk's disapproval of Christmas becoming ever stronger. Instead of it being a day of feasting and celebration, it became an ordinary day of work.

≈ The party's over ≈

Although this move was largely extremely unpopular (and frequently defied), some people in England were very sympathetic to the notion of eradicating Christmas altogether. While the first phase of the English Civil War was raging, the new national liturgy of the Church of England was published in January 1645. It was made plain that Christmas had no place in the life of the Church and was therefore redundant. This became law two years later, to the general dismay of the population. The English were already fed up with the new regime (Charles I was in prison and the Roundheads, under Oliver Cromwell, were in power), which had massively increased taxation to pay for the war, so they were less than thrilled by this stamping out of one of their favourite feasts of the year. Soldiers roamed the streets each Christmas Day, searching out churchgoers who had ignored the ban and anyone else who was observing Christmas in any way at all (including staying at home when they were supposed to be at work). A rhyme of the time made it clear what many people thought of this:

> The high-shoe lords of Cromwell's making
> Were not for dainties – roasting, baking;
> The chiefest food they found most good in,
> Was rusty bacon and bag-pudding;
> Plum-broth was popish, and mince-pie —
> O that was flat idolatry!

❧ The return of Christmas ❧

When Charles II assumed the English throne in 1660, with the Restoration of the monarchy, all legislation that had been passed since 1642 was declared invalid. This meant that Christmas was back on the agenda, and the announcement was greeted with relief by the people who had suffered under the harsh imposition of Puritan law. (Scotland followed suit in 1661.) Samuel Pepys certainly enjoyed himself that December, and his diary entry for 27 December 1660 records 'About the middle of the night I was very ill – I think with eating and drinking too much'.

However, not everyone agreed with the reinstitution of Christmas, and even now some practising Christians – especially Calvinists – do not celebrate it.

JOINING THE GOOSE CLUB

No, a goose club has nothing to do with joining a group of people who enjoy pinching one another's bottoms. At least, that wasn't the main intention, although who knows what everyone got up to when the drink started to flow.

The goose club was the salvation of many a Victorian family's Christmas. At the time, people who could afford it preferred to eat beef or turkey on Christmas Day. Those who couldn't stretch their money that far chose to eat goose, but even this was an expensive option for some. And so the goose club was born. It enabled people who couldn't afford to buy their Christmas food in a single transaction to save a few pence each week, throughout the year, for their Christmas feast (even if 'feast' is an overstatement of what some of them would be eating on the big day). Come Christmas, they would receive a goose and possibly some other treats as well, such as a couple of bottles of gin.

Goose clubs were run by local merchants, such as butchers and grocers, publicans and innkeepers, and a group of friends might get together and form their own goose club too. Sometimes the clubs met frequently, providing the opportunity for some convivial entertainment throughout the year. Naturally, vinegary Victorian do-gooders shook their collective heads at this sign of working-class roistering.

When Christmas arrived and it was time to distribute the bounty to all the members of the club, there was the ticklish problem of sharing out the geese in a way that satisfied everyone. Geese come in a variety of shapes and sizes. Some are plump and juicy birds, while others might look as though they've been on a strict diet and you certainly wouldn't want one of those adorning your Christmas table if you could help it. Allowing all the members of the goose club to grab their chosen bird would undoubtedly have ended in mayhem, with fragments of the choicest geese strewn in all directions, so people drew lots or rolled dice in order to allocate the birds fairly. You might strike poultry gold and take home the fattest bird of all, or you might have to be content with its emaciated shadow. After all, you would console yourself, there was always next year.

THE CHRISTMAS TRUCE

The war was supposed to be over by Christmas 1914. But it wasn't. What eventually became known as the First World War was merely gathering pace. The British, French, Belgian and German soldiers who had enlisted with such fervour only a few months before had already witnessed scenes that turned them from idealists to something much darker and more knowing.

In December 1914, instead of being at home with their families, the British and German soldiers who had survived the slaughter so far were huddled in their respective trenches in France and Flanders. The weather was bitter and the ground was frozen.

The British were on the alert for an attack by the Germans, having been warned about it in a message from General Headquarters on Christmas Eve: 'It is thought possible that the enemy may be contemplating an attack during Xmas or New Year. Special vigilance will be maintained during these periods.' We can imagine the men, tense, nervous, shivering with the cold, and waiting.

What happened next took many of the soldiers by surprise and has never been forgotten. And it happened at various places all along the Western Front, so it wasn't an isolated incident. Some British soldiers saw lights twinkling in the Germans' trenches. These were candles, which the Germans had lit in an attempt to remember that it was Christmas. Other soldiers heard men wishing each other a happy Christmas. And, above all, the guns were silent.

Tentatively, in case it was a trap, soldiers on both sides climbed out of their trenches and ventured across no-man's-land to shake one another's hands and, sometimes, to share their precious cigarettes, chocolate or beer. Many of them agreed to hold a truce throughout Christmas Day, and some also agreed to warn one another before hostilities began again. In some cases, the truce lasted for the whole of Christmas Day and Boxing Day, with guns fired on both sides to indicate that the fighting was about to resume. Amazingly, there are stories of the truce lasting for much longer in some areas. As well as bringing some semblance of normality to what had become hell on earth, the truce also gave the soldiers on both sides a chance to collect their dead from wherever they had fallen and take them back to their lines without being fired on.

One of the most famous incidents of this unofficial truce was a football match between the opposing sides on Christmas Day, on the front line between Frelinghien and Houplines. Using their caps to mark the goalposts, soldiers from the 133rd Royal Saxon Regiment played against men from the Seaforth Highlanders, who amused the Saxons by proving that Scotsmen really don't wear anything underneath their kilts. The men played on the frosty ground for an hour before the German Commanding Officer heard about the match and ordered that it should come to an end. The score was 3–2 to the Germans.

The men who wrote about the truce, regardless of which side they fought on, appreciated it and were touched by it. They were also quick to point out the irony of the good-natured truce being followed by the resumption of violent hostilities.

According to contemporary accounts, the widespread Christmas truce of 1914 was never repeated during the rest of the war. By December 1915 the fighting on both sides had become so bitter, and the level of casualties so great, that most soldiers no longer had the stomach for what could only be a temporary truce.

A MERRY 'MOCK' CHRISTMAS

You needed ingenuity if you wanted to celebrate Christmas in any kind of style during the Second World War. Rationing began in Britain on 8 January 1940 and continued until 4 July 1954 – long after the war was over. By Christmas 1940, when the war had begun to bite and Britain was enduring heavy bombing raids, many foods were scarce. Meat, bacon, butter, margarine and sugar were all rationed during 1940, although the sugar ration was increased from 8 to 12 ounces during the week before Christmas. It could be difficult to find the spare ingredients to make special Christmas foods, assuming that your kitchen was in a fit state to do so after all the air raids. More foods were rationed in 1941, including cheese, eggs and jam. Even worse was to come for children in 1942 when sweets and chocolate were added to the list.

As the war progressed and sometimes even rationed food disappeared from the shelves, people began to save a little bit of their ration weeks ahead of Christmas so they would have something festive to eat. But that required some clever thinking, as vital ingredients often weren't available. The Ministry of Food began to issue recipes for dishes that were intended as delicious alternatives to those that were scarce or unobtainable. These dishes often had 'mock' in their name, which was a big clue that they weren't what they seemed. You could have mock duck, for instance, or mock turkey (made from lamb or mutton and billed as being 'as delicious as any turkey!'), not to mention mock cream and even mock marzipan to put on your mock Christmas cake. For some people, all this made a mockery of the entire business of eating decent food.

By 1943, such Christmas essentials as Christmas puddings were in disappointingly short supply. One commentator wrote for Mass Observation, the social research association: 'We are pretty well on our beam ends as far as Christmas fare is concerned ... A few Christmas puddings are about. There are shops with three puddings and 800 registered customers.'

Any food that was imported was particularly precious and prone to sudden disappearance, as it was transported by ships that ran the risk of being sunk by enemy action. Dried fruit (rationed from January 1942) and sugar, therefore, could be scarce, so other sweet and moist ingredients were added to recipes in their place. Home-made Christmas puddings, for instance, frequently contained grated potatoes, carrots or parsnips during the war – and for some time afterwards, too. Some of these recipes were successful but others were so disgusting that they weren't worth bothering with, especially as they involved valuable rations that could be used in more satisfying ways. People learnt to go without some things and to make do with what they had. Sometimes, the fact that they were still in one piece was reason enough to celebrate.

CHRISTMAS FRUIT PIES

In 1942, when the Second World War seemed endless and strict rationing meant there was little or no chance of having a decent Christmas blow-out, the Ministry of Food published a leaflet of festive recipes that, it claimed, made 'Christmas fare hearty, appetising and tempting to look at'. You will notice there is no mention of what it might taste like. You will also note that it requires dried fruit, although this was rationed and not always available. It would have been a case of grabbing it when you saw it.

This mixture is a good alternative to mincemeat:

Warm 1 tablespoon marmalade (or jam, but this is not so spicy) in small saucepan over tiny heat. Add ¼ lb prunes (soaked 24 hours, stoned, chopped) or other dried fruit, 1 tablespoon sugar, 1 teacupful stale cake crumbs, or half cake, half breadcrumbs, ½ teaspoonful mixed spice. Stir together until crumbs are quite moist. Remove from heat, add 1 large chopped apple; also some chopped nuts if you have any. Make up into small pies, or large open flans. The mixture keeps several days in a cool place.

A HOME-MADE CHRISTMAS

Children who dreamt of waking up to a bulging stocking full of lavish toys on Christmas morning were almost bound to be disappointed during times of hardship. Father Christmas still managed to arrive, despite the privations of war or economic depressions, but the contents of his sack were often obviously home-made.

In her memoir *A Child in the Forest* (later renamed *Full Hearts and Empty Bellies*), Winifred Foley wrote about her childhood in the

Forest of Dean in the 1920s. One Christmas, when the family finances were stretched particularly tight, she longed for Father Christmas to bring her a doll. On Christmas morning, the doll was there but it was made from an old black sock, with unmatched buttons for eyes and red stitching for a mouth. At first, Winifred's bitter disappointment at 'the ugliest apology for a doll one could never hope to see' made her spurn it, but that didn't last long and the doll became her beloved companion until it was ruined in a thunderstorm. At which point she gave it a ceremonial burial.

During the Second World War, shop-bought toys could be ruinously expensive, assuming that you could find them in the first place. Fewer toys were being made because many toy factories had switched production to items that helped the war effort. Parents who had access to the black market and were therefore able to buy toys that were otherwise virtually unobtainable had a greater choice, but they needed deep pockets to pay for such expensive treats. The answer for many parents was to make the toys themselves.

That was all very well but even finding the raw materials for the toys could be tricky. In an era where nothing went to waste and recycling was a way of life and a means of survival, all sorts of oddments were pressed into service. Old stockings, so heavily darned that they couldn't be worn any longer, were stuffed with fabric offcuts and turned into dolls, and the tiny rolls of cotton wool that fitted inside the top of aspirin bottles were far too useful to throw away. Oddments of wood were whittled into the shape of toy cars, boats and planes. Anything with a wartime or patriotic theme was especially popular, including dartboards bearing pictures of Hitler in the bullseye. Kites, however, were frowned upon in case they flew so high that they interfered with British planes or were mistaken for enemy aircraft.

Decorating the house for Christmas was another test of ingenuity. If commercial paper chains weren't available, children could make their own by gluing strips of painted newspaper together. Sweet wrappers and bits of shiny paper were hoarded for months before being carefully smoothed out and cut up to make other decorations. The Ministry of Food, always so eager with its handy hints, suggested filling empty fruit bowls with Christmassy displays of carrots, beetroot and sprigs of parsley. Patriotic this may have been but no doubt many people would have willingly traded a whole bowlful of beetroot for a single juicy tangerine.

TRUSTING
TO LUCK

A sad tale's best for winter.
I have one of sprites and goblins.

A WINTER'S TALE, ACT II, SCENE I, WILLIAM SHAKESPEARE

CHRISTMAS WEATHER

Today, we are most likely to pay attention to the Christmas weather because of fears that it will affect our travel plans, or because we enjoy crossing frozen puddles and hearing the ice crack beneath our feet. But our ancestors set great store by the weather at this time of year because they believed it gave them clues about what the year ahead would bring.

❧ Sunshine ❧

Apple growers in Devon and Derbyshire used to hope for sunshine at Christmas because it boded well for the next harvest. They even had rhyme about it:

If the sun shines through the apple trees upon a Christmas Day,
When autumn comes they will a load of fruit display.

❧ Rain ❧

If it rained a lot during the Twelve Days of Christmas, that was taken as a sign that the following year would be wet too.

❧ Mild temperatures ❧

You might imagine that a mild Christmas would please all those superstitious soothsayers, but not always. According to a not-very-cheery saying, a green Christmas makes a fat churchyard. On a less sombre note, a green Christmas is supposed to ensure a good harvest, so all is not lost if the frost stays away.

❧ Windy weather ❧

It was considered important to take note of the weather on New Year's Eve, because that was thought to indicate what to expect in the coming twelve months.

> If New Year's Eve night-wind blows south,
> It betokeneth warmth and growth;
> If west, much milk, and fish in the sea;
> If north, cold and storms there will be;
> If east, the trees will bear much fruit;
> If north-east, flee it, man and brute!

THE OX AND ASS

It was once widely believed in many parts of Britain, but especially in the countryside, that animals instinctively knew when it was midnight on Christmas Eve. It was said that they responded to this important moment by kneeling down in homage to the newborn Jesus. Some people even believed that the animals were able to speak to each other. Others claimed that cattle turned to the east and bowed.

Strangely enough, these miraculous events have never been verified. Some authorities asserted that it was highly dangerous to witness them, while others claimed that only the most saintly humans were deemed worthy of experiencing them. These saints in mortal form presumably had their own reasons for not revealing whether any of these miraculous events actually happened.

When the Gregorian calendar was introduced in Britain in 1752, provoking much controversy and suspicion, some people chose to use various Christmas customs as a means of discrediting the new calendar. One of these was reported in *Bentley's Magazine* in 1847.

It is said, as the morning of the day on which Christ was born, the cattle in the stalls kneel down; and I have heard it confidently asserted that, when the new style [the Gregorian calendar] came in, the younger cattle only knelt on December 25, while the older bullocks preserved their genuflections for Old Christmas Day, January 6.

Thomas Hardy, who wrote so powerfully of all things bucolic, was moved to write a poem about this in which the narrator looked back with wistful nostalgia to this 'fancy', as he called it.

'Christmas Eve, and twelve of the clock,
Now they are all on their knees,'
An elder said as we sat in a flock
By the embers in the hearthside ease.

We pictured the meek mild creatures where
They dwelt in their strawy pen,
Nor did it occur to one of us there
To doubt they were kneeling then.

So fair a fancy few would weave
In these years! Yet, I feel,
If someone said on Christmas Eve,
'Come, see the oxen kneel

In the lonely barton by yonder coomb
Our children used to know,'
I should go with him in the gloom,
Hoping it might be so.

CHRISTMAS EVE SUPERSTITIONS

Christmas Eve is often a very busy day, especially for those of us who are desperately trying to finish off our Christmas preparations. These can range from crawling around under the tree while decoratively arranging our beautifully wrapped and thoughtfully chosen gifts, each one bearing a gift tag written in the exquisite calligraphy we've been practising for months, to being jostled in an overheated, overcrowded and overpriced shop while we stare at the long list of presents we have yet to buy and go into a complete panic.

For our ancestors, it seems that Christmas Eve was equally busy, but possibly for different reasons. They had so many Christmas Eve traditions to follow that they must have been hard pressed to get any work done.

≈ Apples ≈

If you want to ensure that you will be at the peak of health throughout the coming twelve months, you must eat an apple at midnight on Christmas Eve.

❧ Bees ❧

If you keep bees, you might be tempted to hang about their hives at midnight on Christmas Eve. That's because they will start to hum the tune of the Hundredth Psalm, which begins, appropriately enough, with 'Make a joyful noise unto the Lord'.

In Yorkshire, bee-keepers were once encouraged to talk to their bees on Christmas Eve. If the bees hummed in response, it was said to presage a good summer.

❧ Bread ❧

Our ancestors used to believe that any bread baked on Christmas Eve is blessed. It will always bake well, apparently, so there is no fear of blunting your teeth on a heavy loaf, and it also carries healing powers. What is more, keeping the Christmas loaf in your home ensures that the building and its inhabitants are safe from harm. How very fortunate that the Christmas loaf apparently has the miraculous ability of staying fresh from one Christmas to the next, thereby ruling out any danger of food poisoning.

Another superstition maintains that it is lucky to leave a loaf of bread on the table on Christmas Eve because it guarantees a plentiful supply of bread in the following year.

❧ Dumb cakes ❧

Any single woman who wanted to know who she was going to marry was once advised to do some baking late on Christmas Eve. But not any ordinary baking. She had to make what was known as a 'dumb cake', because she baked it in silence. The ingredients were equal proportions of salt, wheatmeal and barley, which she fashioned into a flat cake. She would put the cake in the oven shortly before midnight and leave the front door open. At midnight, her future husband would enter the house and turn the cake over in the oven. Folklore remains silent about what the woman was supposed to do if she was disappointed about the identity of the man who crossed the threshold.

A tradition from the Cotswolds involved the single woman pricking her initials in the top of the cake. When her husband-to-be turned up at midnight, he was supposed to prick his initials next to hers on the cake, and then she had to take the cake out of the oven and eat it. It is interesting to note that she was the only one allowed to eat the cake. It must have tasted disgusting, thanks to its high proportion of salt, so if her intended had eaten it too it would almost undoubtedly have raised doubts about her culinary skills. Having gone to all the trouble of enticing a man into her home in the first place, she wouldn't want him to rush out again in a tearing hurry.

≈ Farming ≈

Christmas Eve is apparently such a holy day that any seed sown in the soil will germinate, even if the ground is sodden from too much rain or has frozen solid.

≈ Fruit trees ≈

It pays to look after your fruit trees on Christmas Eve if you want to ensure a plentiful crop in the coming year. One way to do this is to tie a stone to a branch of each fruit tree. Alternatively, you can wrap wet straw around its trunk.

≈ Hay ≈

Feeding hay to your farm animals can be an expensive business. If you want to reduce your feed bill during the next twelve months, yet still have cattle that fatten up well, you should carry some hay around your local church three times on Christmas Eve. But do make sure you carry it in a clockwise direction, because carrying it widdershins (anticlockwise) will conjure up the Devil.

≈ Hoops-a-daisy ≈

You have to keep a watchful eye over any wine or beer casks that might be in the house on Christmas Eve. If one of the hoops that hold the cask together should fall off on this most important night, it means that someone in the house is going to die.

≈ Mistletoe bough ≈

Mistletoe, which is a most mysterious plant because of all the legends and myths that surround it, was once believed to protect houses from fires and lightning strikes. A Christmas bough, made from mistletoe, was often kept in the house all year, only being replaced when the new Christmas decorations were brought in on the following Christmas Eve. In some parts of England, this tradition was practised at midnight on New Year's Eve, and the old bough was taken outside and immediately burnt.

≈ Straw ≈

For some farming people, there was a strong connection between the manger in which the infant Christ was laid and the manger from which their own cattle ate. It was considered lucky to give each of your cattle a strand of straw at Christmas.

CHRISTMAS SPIRITS

Although evenings spent sitting round the festive fireside in convivial company are often an invitation to tell deliciously shivery ghost stories and other tales of things that go bump in the night, the spirits themselves are traditionally very quiet at Christmas. It is said that the holy nature of Christmas prevents the activity of any malevolent spirits, but judging by the following stories it seems that the supernatural realms fail to completely vanish at this time of year. If you don't believe this, ask Ebenezer Scrooge to tell you about the most memorable Christmas Eve he ever spent.

✒ King Arthur ✒

Apparently King Arthur, the legendary (some would say 'mythical') king who is said to be sleeping until his country once again needs him, leads a procession of his knights through Somerset each Christmas Eve. They progress from Cadbury Castle, along the track known as Hunting Causeway or Arthur's Lane, to Glastonbury Tor. One tradition has it that they are enjoying what is known as the Wild Hunt (a mythological hunt that the Teutonic god Wotan also took part in), and that they also hunt on Midsummer's Eve and Midsummer's Night. It is said that even if you can't see the knights themselves, you may hear the thundering of their horses' hooves and the baying of their excited dogs.

✒ Returning souls ✒

Our ancestors maintained that it was essential to get the house spick and span before leaving for church on Christmas morning. All the food should already have been prepared for the Christmas feast, with the kitchen looking neat and tidy. While the family was at church, it was believed that the spirits of dead members of the family would return to their old home to have a good look round it so they could check that everything was in order. They might even have something to eat before departing again. If they were pleased with what they found, they would confer good fortune on the household for the coming year. If they were less than chuffed with the mess, the consequences didn't bear thinking about.

❧ The gates of Paradise ❧

According to Irish belief, the gates of Paradise are opened wide at midnight on Christmas Eve, so that the soul of anyone who has just died automatically enters the kingdom of heaven – with no questions asked by St Peter, presumably.

SOWEN CAKES

An old tradition in Scotland kept people busy before the sun was up on Christmas morning. They would boil up the inner husks from oats (known as sids) in some water until the mixture had turned into a sort of thick soup. The next step was to drain off the oaty liquid and keep it in readiness for drinking at Hogmanay. What remained was made into cakes and baked.

Each member of the family would be given one of these sowen cakes. They had to keep it intact before eating it at the big Christmas feast that evening. If it survived in one piece, whoever the sowen cake belonged to could look forward to plenty of happiness. But if the cake broke, so did any chances of joy for its owner.

MINCE PIE ETIQUETTE

So many superstitions surround the consumption of mince pies at Christmas that perhaps we should talk about mince pie eatiquette instead of etiquette.

❧ No knives, please ❧

Never, ever, cut a mince pie with a knife. You will be courting bad luck in the most foolhardy way. Break it up with a fork or spoon, or simply pick it up and take a big bite.

❧ Make a wish! ❧

When you are about to eat the first mince pie of the Christmas season, don't unthinkingly shove it in your mouth. You must make a wish first. Exactly when you eat this first mince pie is, of course, entirely a matter of personal preference. It might be when mince pies first appear in the shops, which could be anytime from late autumn, or it might be when you put up your Christmas tree. If you want to hedge your bets and play safe, perhaps you could make a wish every time you eat a mince pie.

❧ One a day ❧

Soothsayers from the past used to advise eating a mince pie on each of the Twelve Days of Christmas. Apparently this will guarantee a happy year to come.

❧ Only a fool would refuse ❧

This next superstition is really bad news for anyone who dislikes mince pies, because it decrees that no one who is offered a mince pie over Christmas should refuse it. It has nothing to do with the fear of offending your host or hostess (even though that might happen) but because you will be declining good fortune when you say no to the pie. This rule applies even if you are already full to bursting with all the mince pies you've eaten in other houses on the same day.

❧ Shhh! ❧

Mince pies should always be eaten in silence. This is a rule that is easy to keep if you are eating while desperately trying to remember all the things you should be doing to court good fortune.

THE LITTLE PEOPLE

As you might expect from an age-old festival whose roots are partly buried in pagan soil, fairies, elves, gnomes and other 'little people' have played a role in the Christmas festivities.

⇒ I can see you! ⇐

Most mortals find it impossible to see fairies and other elementals. However, if you want to try, apparently there are certain times of the year when it's easier to spot them. The evening of a full moon, between twilight and midnight, is always a good bet. You also stand a better chance of spotting the little people on Lady Day (25 March, which is the Feast of the Annunciation and until 1752 was officially New Year's Day in Britain), May Day (1 May), Midsummer's Day (24 June), Hallowe'en (31 October) and Christmas Day.

⇒ Pax! ⇐

It was once believed that even if the human world and that of the elementals were in conflict for the majority of the year, they called a truce at Christmastime. The woodland fairies, sprites, pixies and other creatures were thought to live in deciduous trees each summer. But when the trees dropped their leaves in autumn, the elementals would take shelter in evergreens, such as holly, yew and ivy. When humans picked these evergreens to decorate their homes over Christmas, they brought the elementals indoors with them.

Most humans would think twice before knowingly doing anything so reckless as to bring an elemental indoors because you never knew what a mischievous sprite might get up to, but all was well over Christmas because of the truce. The moment the truce ended, however (which was originally Candlemas and later Twelfth Night), the greenery had to taken outside before its tiny residents got up to any tricks. Some traditions state that all the greenery should then be burnt, which seems unfair to the fairies. We can only hope that they were able to escape the flames in good time.

FROM CHRISTMAS TO CANDLEMAS

These days, our Christmas decorations usually go up in our homes at some point in December. It's different for shops, of course, which often like to anticipate Christmas by decking themselves out in trees, baubles and fake snow in early September, thus coinciding with a late summer heatwave.

❧ Down they come! ❧

But when should the decorations come down again? Modern tradition tells us that they must vanish on Twelfth Night to avoid bad luck. Unfortunately, identifying this important date isn't as easy as it seems. Our forebears knew it as 5 January, and it was followed by Twelfth Day, which was the last of the Twelve Days of Christmas. Nowadays, we consider Twelfth Night to be 6 January. Let's hope that the bad luck is aware of this confusion and isn't waiting to swoop down on anyone whose tree and cards are still in place on the morning of the 6th.

❧ Wait for Candlemas ❧

Between the seventeenth and nineteenth centuries it would have been considered indecently early, not to mention foolish in the extreme (once again because of the bad luck that would follow), to dismantle our decorations on Twelfth Night. The evergreen decorations picked from our gardens and woods went up on Christmas Eve and there they stayed – regardless of how tatty they became – until

Candlemas, which is 2 February. Even now, some churches in Britain still uphold this custom of holding on to the Christmas decorations until Candlemas.

There is an important connection between Christmas Day and Candlemas, which celebrates the purification of the Virgin Mary forty days after she gave birth to Jesus, and also the presentation of Jesus to God in the temple. In the days when the only means of illumination was candlelight, all the candles that would be burned in the coming year were blessed – hence the name of the day. In pre-Christian times, 2 February was celebrated as the halfway point between the winter solstice and the spring equinox, and was a festival of light. The light was the light of the sun. When Christianity absorbed the festival into its own calendar, the light became that of Jesus, who said 'I am the light of the world' (John 9:5).

❧ Disposing of the evergreens ❧

As is often the case with traditions, there were conflicting ideas about what was supposed to happen to the wilted and dusty decorations when they came down at Candlemas. Some people took everything outside and burnt it. It was widely believed that elves, fairies and other little folk were so attracted by the greenery that there was a strong chance they'd take up residence in it, and the only way to dispose of these dangerous creatures was with cleansing fire. As a result, every scrap of leaf and berry had to be burnt until it was reduced to ash. But not everyone agreed with this rule. Some either disposed of the greenery by feeding it to their livestock or they left it to rot down outside. Presumably, the little folk hopped off it at this point and returned to their original homes.

It was essential that every last scrap of the Christmas evergreens in churches was removed at Candlemas. In an era when every churchgoer had their own position in a pew, it was commonly believed that any sign of this festive greenery in a pew come Candlemas meant certain death before the end of the year for that position's inhabitant. The temptation to strike fear in the heart of the most hated member of the congregation by leaving a single holly berry on their seat must, at times, have been almost overwhelming.

HIGH JINKS

Wonderful party, wonderful games, wonderful
unanimity, won-der-ful happiness!

A CHRISTMAS CAROL, CHARLES DICKENS

BULLET PUDDING

It's tempting to imagine that people in Regency times spent their days sitting on overstuffed sofas making polite conversation while sipping cups of tea. But they also knew how to enjoy themselves. And, it seems, sometimes they did so in what we might consider rather dangerous ways.

One favourite Regency party game, which Jane Austen's family enjoyed each Christmas, was called 'bullet pudding'. It had nothing to do with anyone's disastrous cooking, as might be imagined. Fanny Austen, who was Jane's niece, described the game in a rather hectic manner in a letter dated 17 January 1804.

> You must have a large pewter dish filled with flour which you must pile up into a sort of pudding with a peek [peak] at top. You must then lay a bullet [yes, a real bullet] at top and everybody cuts a slice of it [the pudding], and the person that is cutting it when it [the bullet] falls must poke about with their noses and chins till they find it and then take it out with their mouths which makes them strange figures all covered with flour but the worst is that you must not laugh for fear of the flour getting up your nose and mouth and choking you: You must not use your hands in taking the Bullet out.

One can only wonder at what anyone connected with health and safety regulations would have had to say on the matter, not only because of the possibility of being asphyxiated by the flour but also the recklessness of playing with live ammunition. So don't try this at home, boys and girls.

SNAPDRAGON

S itting in the dark, with only a few flames to light the room, can be a magical experience. One traditional Christmas game, which was often played on Christmas Eve, made the most of this. It was called snapdragon.

After everyone had finished eating, a wide dish, piled high with almonds, raisins and other dried fruit, was placed in the centre of the table. It was doused in warmed brandy, the lights in the room were extinguished and then someone set light to the brandy. The point of the game was for everyone to dart their hand into the flames, snatch hold of some of the dried fruit (the quicker the better) and eat it. And then they did it all over again until there was none left. Sometimes they sang a song, which describes the perils of the game, at the same time.

> Here he comes with flaming bowl,
> Don't be mean to take his toll,
> Snip! Snap! Dragon!
>
> Take care you don't take too much,
> Be not greedy in your clutch,
> Snip! Snap! Dragon!
>
> With his blue and lapping tongue
> Many of you will be stung,
> Snip! Snap! Dragon!
>
> For he snaps at all that comes
> Snatching at his feast of plums,
> Snip! Snap! Dragon!
>
> But Old Christmas makes him come,
> Though he looks so fee! fa! fum!
> Snip! Snap! Dragon!

Don't 'ee fear him, be but bold –
Out he goes, his flames are cold,
Snip! Snap! Dragon!

Snapdragon was wildly popular between the sixteenth and early twentieth centuries, and is mentioned by many writers including William Shakespeare (who called it 'flap-dragon'), Jane Austen, Anthony Trollope and Charles Dickens, but it has almost disappeared now for obvious reasons of safety.

PARTY PIECES

Back in the days before television, radio and what was once called the gramophone, everyone had to make their own amusement in the evenings, and Christmas was no exception. Many people made a special effort at this time of year, and even those elderly aunts and uncles who would rather have had a quiet snooze in a comfortable chair would force themselves to join in – and then find they were enjoying themselves so much they were laughing loudest of all.

Joyful, heartfelt laughter is one of the most important elements of a happy Christmas, and getting the entire family involved in some old-fashioned games (often the simpler the better) is one of the best ways of ensuring that everyone has a really good time.

❧ Blind man's buff ❧

There is almost no limit to the number of people who can play this game, but it helps to have a large room if there are lots of participants. It is also a wise precaution to remove any fragile or valuable objects before the game begins, as well as any furniture that could turn the game into a treacherous obstacle course that ends with a trip to the nearest A & E department.

One person is chosen as 'it' and is blindfolded with a scarf. They stand in the middle of the room and turn round three times, then blunder about trying to touch the people who are dancing out of their way. Anyone who is caught by 'it' has to retire from the game. The game finishes either when everyone has been caught or (to save potential boredom) when a set time limit has elapsed. The last person to be caught then becomes 'it'.

❧ Charades ❧

In smart circles, this is known as 'The Game'. Versions of it are often played on television, too. Regardless of what you choose to call it, charades relies on rudimentary acting ability, a few wild leaps of imagination and a sense of humour.

One person is chosen as 'it' and thinks of a phrase, such as a proverb or cliché, or the title of a book, film or play, which they can act out. They then have to mime which category their choice belongs to and hold up their fingers to show how many words the phrase contains. Then they act it out, perhaps acting out each syllable if it's one word, or acting out each word in turn. Alternatively, they might act out what the phrase means. While they're doing this, the rest of the group guesses what the phrase might be and shouts out suggestions. The person who comes up with the correct answer then becomes 'it'.

∾ Consequences ∾

During a series of party games, you always reach the stage of needing to sit down and recover your breath. Consequences is the perfect game to play while everyone is getting their second wind. Each person is given a sheet of paper and a pen. Someone reads out a set of questions about two people meeting and what happens between them. Each player writes the answer to the first question on their piece of paper. Then they fold down the top flap of the paper to hide their answer and pass the paper on to their right-hand neighbour. They then write the answer to the second question on the new piece of paper they've been given, before folding it over as before and passing it on. And so it continues until the end of the questions. Then everyone unfolds their sheet of paper and reads out the answers, which are often so funny because of the collision of different stories that everyone is reduced to helpless laughter.

The questions can vary, but these offer plenty of opportunity for fun. Here is a simple version, although you can expand it with more questions. He [you write a man's name] meets she [you write a woman's name] at [you write down where they met]. He says to her [you write down what he says]. She says to him [you write down what she says]. The consequence is [you write down what happened between them]. And the world says [this is often answered by writing down a well-known phrase].

∾ Hunt the thimble ∾

All you need for this is a thimble (you can use some other small object if you don't have a thimble) and at least two players. Everyone is shown the object that they must hunt for, then they leave the room and the player who has been designated 'it' hides the thimble somewhere in the room (such as behind a cushion or on top of a bookcase). When 'it' is ready, the players return to the room and walk around it, hunting the thimble. 'It' has to guide them by calling out 'warm' when they get near the thimble, 'hot' when they're closer still, 'boiling hot' when they're almost on top of it, and so on. Equally, they call out 'cold' or 'frozen' as a player gets further away from the thimble. The person who finds the thimble first becomes 'it'.

Kim's game

This simple game gets its name from Rudyard Kipling's novel *Kim*, in which the main character has to play it during his training as a spy. One person arranges a selection of between ten and fifteen assorted objects on a tray and covers it with a large cloth. They carry it into the room where all the other players are waiting, each equipped with paper and pen. Then the cloth is removed from the tray and each player has to study it for one minute before the cloth is replaced and the tray removed. Each player has to scribble down as many of the objects as they can remember. The winner is the person who has named the greatest number of objects.

Pass the parcel

This game requires some forward planning but it's worth it because most people enjoy it – probably because it takes them back to their childhoods. The organiser buys a small prize, such as a box of chocolates, and wraps it in at least eight layers of paper. It helps to use paper of a different colour or pattern for each layer, so these are easily distinguished. The organiser can put a tiny gift or a piece of paper bearing a forfeit (such as 'dance on the spot for one minute') between each layer to make the game more interesting.

Everyone sits in a circle and the organiser plays some music while the players pass the parcel in a clockwise direction. When the music stops, the person holding the parcel unwraps a layer of paper and either keeps the gift concealed within the layer or performs the forfeit. Then the music resumes and the parcel is passed round again until the music stops once more, when the next layer of paper is unwrapped. And so it goes on until the last person holding the parcel when the music stops unwraps the prize.

Small children particularly love this game but they do need supervising. There is always a chance of disputes over who is holding the parcel when the music stops, and it's good to make sure that the music stops in such a way that each player gets at least one chance to unwrap the parcel and receive a gift or forfeit. Otherwise, what you had intended to be an enjoyable game could end in a tantrum. And as for the children's reactions…

CHRISTMAS CARDS

The history of playing cards is a fascinating and somewhat contentious topic. There are plenty of theories about who invented them and which country they came from, including the notion that they originated in China, but the facts are vague. Even so, the consequences of card games were already causing trouble in Europe in the fourteenth century, and so playing cards were duly banned in Florence and Paris. In some places, the only time of year when you could play cards was at Christmas.

Early packs of cards were beautifully decorated by hand, but commercial production in mainland Europe had begun by the start of the fifteenth century. No one knows when playing cards first arrived in England but they were mentioned in what are known as the Paston letters, which is a collection of letters exchanged between members of the Paston family between 1422 and 1509. These letters are invaluable for shedding light on some of the customs and mores of the time. In one of the letters, John Paston replies to his wife Margaret's question about the pastimes that their widowed neighbour could allow in her home over Christmas. He tells Margaret that dancing was not permissible but cards and chess were.

In his first Parliament, held between 1461 and 1462, Edward IV banned dicing (betting with dice) and the playing of cards, although they were allowed during the Twelve Days of Christmas. Henry VII did something similar in 1495–6 when he decreed that servants could only play cards during the Twelve Days of Christmas, and only in their own homes, to boot.

MUMMERS

For centuries, one of the seasonal entertainments was mumming. This involved people clad in special costumes who would visit houses on foot and entertain the household in return for some money and possibly something to eat and drink.

It was once commonly believed that mumming owed its origins to pagan fertility rites that flourished in Britain long before Christianity booed them offstage. However, that theory is now thought to be wrong, making mumming a much more recent tradition. It also appears that there were two forms of mumming in the past, so it helps to sort out which was which.

❧ Medieval mummers ❧

The first reference to mumming, or what was sometimes called 'momerie', comes in the thirteenth century, after it spread from mainland Europe to Britain. It involved troupes of entertainers dressed in outlandish costumes, including elaborate masks and animal heads, who would dance and sing in villages and towns. Mumming grew in popularity, and mummers entertained Edward III and his court during the Christmas of 1347.

Mumming was a wonderful entertainment and curiosity for some people, but for others it was all rather dangerous. Some people took advantage of the disguise that the mumming masks offered and got up to all sorts of unruly and criminal behaviour. So much so, in fact, that mumming was banned in several European cities and then, in 1405, in London too.

Despite these restrictions, mumming survived. It even survived the Puritan clampdown on most types of Christmas fun, though the disguises still offered plenty of opportunities for those who enjoyed stirring up trouble.

⇔ Mummers' plays ⇔

Things changed in the eighteenth century, when mumming, where people turned up wearing elaborate disguise and sang songs, was replaced by mummers who performed plays. The mummers were still in disguise (hence their alternative name of 'guisers') and, naturally, this still led to punch-ups and thieving. Some people loved them but others were less sanguine. In 1864, a Northamptonshire writer made their feelings plain when they said, 'in this age of refinement few only will allow their dwellings to be the scene of this antic pastime, as the performers enter uninvited, suddenly throwing open the door, and one after the other act their different parts.'

The mummers' plays were performed in simple fashion, with the players often standing in a semi-circle. When it was someone's turn to speak he (it was always a 'he', even if he was dressed as a she) would step forward and then step back into line when he'd finished. The characters usually introduced themselves when they began to speak, usually by saying 'In comes I,' and then giving their character's name.

These were stock characters, and they included the hero, usually a King or Saint George, his antagonist (sometimes a knight or a soldier) and a quack doctor. Another player, called the presenter, was the master of ceremonies. He frequently appeared as Father Christmas, with the words:

> In comes I, Old Father Christmas
> Am I welcome or am I not
> I hope Old Christmas
> Will never be forgot.

As with medieval mumming, the mummers were rewarded with something to eat or drink and, perhaps more importantly, with money. Some low-paid men found that mumming was considerably more profitable than their day jobs.

Mummers' plays fell out of fashion after the First World War but they began to enjoy a revival in the 1960s that has continued ever since. Today, the mummers are more likely to collect money for a charity than for themselves when they bring entertainment to villages during the Christmas season.

OH, NO, IT ISN'T!

Wfalhat would Christmas be without a pantomime? This pantomime is not the sort of chaos that ensues in many households on Christmas morning, when present-opening competes with potato-peeling and the toddler eats all the chocolates, but the theatrical event in which women dress as men and men dress as women, and there's a beginning, a muddle and a rousingly noisy ending.

❧ The history of pantomimes ❧

The roots of British pantomimes go back centuries. Pantos have connections with medieval mummers' plays and also with the Italian *commedia dell'arte* that first arrived in Britain in the sixteenth century. The Italian productions featured their own characters such as the young lovers, Harlequin and Colombine, and Colombine's stern father, Pantaloon. The trouble was that most of the Italian actors couldn't speak much English, so they relied on the sort of comic stage business that we now call slapstick – and which is such an essential element of today's pantomimes. Someone has got to get a custard pie in the face, or fall smack on their bottom, at some point in the production.

The plots of these early Harlequinades, as they were known, bore little resemblance to the pantomimes we know today. But this began to change in the late eighteenth century, when characters that we now recognise, such as Jack the Giant Killer (better known today as the Jack involved with a gigantic beanstalk), began to enter the stories.

Harlequinades embarked on a new chapter in 1800, thanks to a British-born clown called Joseph Grimaldi. The public adored his performances, which featured singing, acrobatics, audience participation and cross-dressing. He had to retire in 1823 because of ill health, but he had set the tone for the pantomimes that were to follow.

The first British pantomime (meaning that it followed a strict set of pantomime conventions, including audience participation, cross-dressing and a pantomime dame played by a man) was *Jack and the Beanstalk*, performed at the Theatre Royal, Drury Lane, London, in 1819. Many others followed, based on fables or fairytales, and all featuring a goodie who's pitched against a baddie, plus a pair of young (and innocent) lovers.

∾ Do join in! ∾

Although most theatrical performers would be horrified if the audience joined in, it's a different story in pantomimes because audience participation is essential, not only in terms of fun but because it is part of what officially makes a pantomime. In fact, a silent audience at a panto would make everyone wonder what on earth had gone wrong. For many children, a trip to the Christmas panto is their first taste of live theatre, so it's got to be as magical as possible.

Members of the audience are expected to laugh uproariously at the jokes, which have to be funny enough to amuse the children while also being clever and topical enough (often larded with plenty of double entendres) to entertain their parents. But instead of sitting in a spellbound and reverent silence when something awful is about to happen to one of the characters, the audience is expected to warn that character by yelling 'It's behind you!' or something similar. The audience boos and hisses whenever the baddie appears, and also disagrees with various statements by shouting out 'Oh, no, it isn't!' or 'Oh, yes, it is!' And they must also be happy to join in the singing because there is usually at least one communal song, with a massive song sheet to remind everyone of the words.

～ The Nutcracker ～

Another traditional and much-loved Christmas performance that involves music is a magical ballet. This is *The Nutcracker*, with music by Peter Tchaikovsky and original choreography by Marius Petipa and Lev Ivanov. It was first performed at the Imperial Mariinksy Theatre in St Petersburg, in Russia, on 18 December 1892, and has since become a staple in the Christmas repertoire of ballet companies around the world. One of the most loved pieces from it is 'The Dance of the Sugar Plum Fairy'.

The plot is based on a story called 'The Nutcracker and the King of Mice' by E F A Hoffman, but the ballet that we love today comes from revisions made to that story in 1844 by the noted French author Alexander Dumas. It is set on a snowy Christmas Eve and features a young girl called Clara and her nutcracker doll.

～ Peter Pan ～

One other theatrical production scores a big hit each Christmas. In common with pantomimes, it relies on some audience participation, especially when one of the characters asks the audience if they believe in fairies. This is *Peter Pan*, JM Barrie's play about a small boy who wouldn't grow up. It was first performed at the Duke of York's Theatre, London, on 27 December 1904. The audience, which consisted mostly of adults decked out in their very best evening clothes, didn't know what to expect and were stunned to discover they were watching what appeared to be a children's story. But they loved it. When the actress playing Tinker Bell asked the audience if they believed in fairies, the response was so powerful and heartfelt that she burst into tears. That production of *Peter Pan* continued to play to packed houses until 1 April 1905, but it was back that December (when a production also opened in New York for the first time), and has been a cherished staple of Christmas theatrical productions ever since.

CHRISTMAS
ON PAPER

25th … After dinner to church again, my wife
and I, where we had a dull sermon of a stranger,
which made me sleep.

THE DIARY OF SAMUEL PEPYS [25 DECEMBER 1660]

WINTER

Many writers have described the sights and sensations of winter, but one of the most evocative is this poem by William Shakespeare, which comes at the end of his play *Love's Labour's Lost*.

The roasted crabs mentioned in the second verse are roasted crab apples, which were often served piping hot in bowls of wassail. We can only hope that greasy Joan was nowhere near at the time.

> When icicles hang by the wall,
> And Dick the shepherd blows his nail,
> And Tom bears logs into the hall,
> And milk comes frozen home in pail,
> When blood is nipp'd and ways be foul,
> Then nightly sings the staring owl—
>   To-who;
> Tu-whit, to-who, a merry note,
> While greasy Joan doth keel the pot.
>
> When all about the wind doth blow,
> And coughing drowns the parson's saw,
> And birds sit brooding in the snow,
> And Marion's nose looks red and raw,
> When roasted crabs hiss in the bowl,

Then nightly sings the staring owl—
   To-who;
Tu-whit, to-who, a merry note,
While greasy Joan doth keel the pot.

ONE BOY'S CHRISTMAS

Those of us who enjoyed happy Christmases as children often look back on them with affection in later years. Charles Lamb, the nineteenth-century essayist and poet, was no exception when he wrote his essay about his schooldays in 'Reflections of Christ's Hospital'.

> Let me have leave to remember the festivities at Christmas, when the richest of us would club our stock to have a gaudy day, sitting round the fire, replenished to the height with logs, and the pennyless, and he that could contribute nothing, partook in all the mirth, and in some of the substantialities of the feasting; the carol sung by night at that time of the year, which, when a young boy, I have so often lain awake to hear from seven (the hour of going to bed) till ten when it was sung by the older boys and monitors, and have listened to it, in their rude chaunting, till I have been transported in fancy to the fields of Bethlehem, and the song which was sung at that season, by angels' voices to the shepherds.

AT THE POULTERER'S

Judging by contemporary accounts, Victorian shops brimmed with a lavish profusion of Christmas foodstuffs. We might imagine that Christmas has only become commercialised in recent years, but it was clearly already a gift to shopkeepers in 1851, when Charles Manby Smith wrote about a London Christmas. Here is his description of the interior of a poulterer's:

Verily, the whole house is feathered like one huge bird, the fabulous roc of the Arabian Tales. The list of them defies all our skill in ornithology. Numbers there are that we know, and as many that are strangers to us – at least with their feathers on. Over the door is a pair of enormous swans, though we do not see the albatross, measuring nine feet across the wings, which we saw in the same place a couple of years back. Above the swans are bitterns, herons, hawks; here a peacock, and there a gigantic crane, besides a raven, and an eccentric collection of birds never intended to be eaten, but which are only hung up aloft to impress the spectator with the indisputable fact, that the whole of the tribes of the air are under the potent enchantment and subject to the despotic beck and bidding of Mr Pluck – and very proper too. Grouse, pheasants, partridges, and wild-fowl hang in countless numbers from the topmost floor down to the very pavement; pigeons in dense dead flocks; and snipes, thrushes, and larks bundled together by the neck in bulky tassels, fringe the solid breast-work of plucked geese and turkeys, which, with heads dangling in silent rows, lie close jammed in fleshy phalanx upon the groaning shop-boards. Hares in legions, and rabbits by the warren, line the walls or hang from the ceiling; and among them here and there the bright feathers of the mallard give a touch of colour to the dense masses of brown and gray.

DEAR DIARY

There is something so exciting and expectant about a pristine new diary, its empty pages waiting to be filled with what you hope will be a fascinating mixture of enjoyable events, delightful social gatherings, memorable meetings and other essential dates to keep you occupied throughout the year ahead. A new diary promises so much and is a good reason to look forward to the coming year.

And, of course, you can write down your list of New Year's resolutions, which you really will keep this year, instead of abandoning them in early January as you've done every other year. This time it's going to be different!

≈ From journal to diary ≈

Until the early 1800s, there was no such thing as a printed diary with a space allocated for each day of the year. Anyone who felt like it recorded their thoughts in a journal – a plain notebook in which they could write as much or as little as they liked, every day if they chose or whenever the spirit moved them. According to the diary company Letts & Co, the first commercial diary was produced by its founder, John Letts, in London in 1812. The venture was so successful that the company began selling printed diaries, similar to today's, in the 1820s.

One person's diary can be a dull affair, full of mundane details or dreary appointments, while another's might be completely gripping. As Gwendolyn Fairfax says in Oscar Wilde's play *The Importance of Being Earnest*, 'I never travel without my diary. One should always have something sensational to read in the train.'

Luckily, some of these diaries have made it into print. They may not be sensational in the way Gwendolyn Fairfax meant, but they give us a fascinating insight into other people's lives and times. Some of the most intriguing British diarists over the centuries include the Reverend Francis Kilvert, Virginia Woolf, Harold Nicolson, Alan Clark, Henry 'Chips' Channon, James Lees-Milne and Frances Partridge. Some other names stand out, too.

John Evelyn

There are two notable diarists from the seventeenth century. One is John Evelyn, a writer and gardener, whose diaries spanned the tumultuous period from 1641–1706. Here is his entry for Christmas Day 1657, when it was against the law to attend church. Not that Evelyn took any notice of that.

> I went with my Wife &c. to *Lond*: to celebrate *Christmas day*. Mr *Gunning* preaching in *Excester* Chapell on 7: *Micha* 2. Sermon Ended, as he was giving us the holy Sacrament, The Chapell was surrounded with Souldiers: All the Communicants and Assembly surpriz'd & kept Prisoners by them, some in the house, others carried away: It fell to my share to be confined to a roome in the house, where yet were permitted to Dine with the master of it, the Countesse of *Dorset*, *Lady Hatton* & some others of quality who invited me: In the afternoone came *Collonel Whaly*, Goffe & others from *Whitehall* to examine us one by one, & some they committed to the *Martial*, some to Prison, some Committed.

Samuel Pepys

The other famous seventeenth-century diarist is Samuel Pepys, who was a civil servant in London. He bought himself a plain paper-covered notebook in December 1659, in readiness for keeping a journal from 1 January 1660. Pepys rose to a high position in the Admiralty, giving us a ringside seat at some of the most notable events of the 1660s, including the Plague of 1665 and the Great Fire of London in 1666. He loved recording the day's events in his diary, which he wrote in shorthand (his wife, Elizabeth, would have been furious if she'd read some of the entries describing his extramarital exploits) and only stopped writing it in December 1669 because he believed (wrongly, as it turned out) that he was going blind.

Pepys frequently liked to enjoy himself, but during Christmas 1664 it sounds as though it was his wife who was having most of the fun:

27th ... a great feast, and good discourse and merry, and so home to bed, where my wife and people innocently at cards, very merry. I to bed, leaving them to their sport and blindman's-buff.

28th ... I went to bed, leaving my wife, and all her folks, and Will also, to come to make Christmas gambols to-night.

29th ... My wife to bed at eight o'clock in the morning, which vexed me a little, but I believe there was no hurt in it at all, but only mirth.

☙ Parson Woodforde ❧

Unlike Pepys, some diarists are celebrated for the glimpses they give us of their more modest lives. Parson James Woodforde wrote almost daily entries in his diary for more than forty years, from 1759–1802. Some of his descriptions of Christmas remind us of what life was like in the days before even the most rudimentary central heating. Here is his diary entry for 28 December (Holy Innocents' Day, which was always regarded as a malign day) 1798:

Frost last night & this Morning & all the Day intense ... Even the Meat in our Pantry all froze & also our bread.

☙ Mr Pooter ❧

Not every celebrated diarist is real. The self-important Charles Pooter was a tireless recorder of his suburban middle-class Victorian life at The Laurels in Holloway, London, as related in *The Diary of a Nobody* by George and Weedon Grossmith. Although it was first published in book form in 1892, it remains one of the great English works of humour.

Poor old Mr Pooter himself was sadly lacking in the humour department, although he did once wake himself up several times in the night laughing at a joke he'd made earlier that evening. But he was certainly a figure of fun to many of the people who knew him, as he discovered on Christmas Eve.

December 24 I am a poor man but I would gladly give ten shillings to find out who sent me the insulting Christmas card I received this morning.

❧ Adrian Mole ❧

It would be impossible to forget another favourite diarist who, admittedly, is once again fictional but whose diaries have added greatly to the gaiety of the nation since they first made it into print in 1982. Adrian Mole's first 'secret' diary was published, with the help of author Sue Townsend, when he was 13¾. Happily for his fans, he has continued to publish his diaries and long may he continue to do so.

In his first diary, he described the romance of exchanging Christmas gifts with Pandora, his then girfriend. He gave her a necklace from Woolworths which she ecstatically believed was solid gold. Unfortunately their date the following day had to be cancelled because a nasty rash had appeared around Pandora's neck. Adrian didn't let on that the necklace had been going cheap.

THE DEAD OF WINTER

What could be cosier at Christmas than lighting the fire, drawing the curtains against the dark night, dimming the lights and re-reading some favourite classic ghost stories? As the logs spit and crack, making you start nervously in your chair – a movement that you pretend is a sudden fit of cramp – you become drawn into the story. It exercises a strangely compulsive spell over you, so that even the twinkling Christmas tree and the cheerful cards on the mantelpiece become tarnished with the faint stain of graveyards, charnel houses and a lurking sense of unease. And even if you congratulate yourself on being unaffected by the creepiest details, they will come back to haunt you later on when you turn out your bedside light and prepare for sleep. Once again you become a child who's convinced that there's something under the bed or hiding behind the curtains. And one who is too scared to investigate.

Some of the best writers of classic ghost stories were Victorians. Sheridan Le Fanu was a renowned writer of gothic horror; his *Carmilla* was the first British novel about vampires. Henry James wrote many full-length novels but one of his most successful works was *The Turn of the Screw* – a ghost story that is still widely read more than one hundred years after it was first published. Charles Dickens loved writing ghost stories and, with his powerful sense of the dramatic, frequently combined them with Christmas settings. He perfectly understood the vivid contrast of the cosily familiar and the sinister unknown.

MR James was another writer who liked to combine his particular brand of creeping supernatural malevolence with an ancient festival, rich in hopes and fears, that is held at the darkest time of the year. Although he was a medieval scholar by profession, MR James is now best known for the ghost stories he wrote, mostly while he was Provost of King's College, Cambridge, and later of Eton College. It became a tradition for him to write a ghost story each December that he would then read aloud, late each Christmas Eve, to a selected group of friends, colleagues and students. It was all highly enjoyable, but it's doubtful that his audience got much sleep afterwards. We can imagine them lying stiffly awake in their cold beds, anxiously alert for unearthly sounds. They were listening for something. And it was unlikely to be Father Christmas.

A DICKENS OF A CHRISTMAS

Nostalgia is nothing new. We've been indulging in it for centuries, if not millennia. And we celebrate the results of one collective bout of nostalgia each December.

In the early nineteenth century, the rise of the Industrial Revolution, which split families and rendered many people out of work when their jobs were mechanised, was having a damaging effect on society. Several notable writers were so concerned about this that they launched an unofficial campaign to rescue Christmas from the doldrums into which it had sunk.

One of these writers was Charles Dickens. He had already dipped his pen into the holly-strewn waters of what he considered to be old-fashioned Christmases when he wrote 'A Christmas Dinner' in his collection of short stories called *Sketches by Boz* (first published in book form in Britain in 1839). Christmas made an even more impressive appearance in Dickens's first novel, *The Posthumous Papers of the Pickwick Club* (first published in book form in 1837), in which Mr Pickwick and his chums spent a splendidly jolly Christmas with the Wardle family at Dingley Dell. *The Pickwick Papers*, as the book was commonly called, was a roaring success. One of the stories within the book concerned a miserable, mercenary sexton called Gabriel Grubb, who had 'a deep scowl of malice and ill-humour'. Grubb was stolen by goblins on Christmas Eve, went through a terrible time and became a changed man. This was a theme Dickens returned to a few years later, with extraordinary results.

Dickens had a keen social conscience (his life was profoundly affected by his own difficult childhood, during which his father was sent to a debtors' prison) and was outraged by the many injustices he saw around him. He was particularly furious about the cruel plight and treatment of impoverished children in Victorian Britain, and in 1843 he was compelled to write a pamphlet on the subject.

He wanted to 'strike a sledge hammer blow' on behalf of the poor. But after mulling this over for some time, Dickens felt it would be far more effective to convey his message through a highly readable, heartstring-tugging Christmas story.

The idea for *A Christmas Carol* came to Dickens while he was staying in Manchester in October 1843. Never a man to hold back when it came to writing, he found that the story poured out of him. He later said that while writing it he 'wept and laughed, and wept again'. He finished it in six weeks, and it was published (at his own expense, as he was in dispute with his publishers at the time) on 19 December that same year. Interestingly, 1843 was also the year when Sir Henry Cole produced his first Christmas card. The sales of *A Christmas Carol* were highly satisfactory: six thousand copies, priced at five shillings each, were sold by Christmas Eve. Dickens hoped to make a good profit on the book but was disappointed, thanks to a combination of various initial printing problems, high production costs (the book was lavishly produced) and, from January 1844, the appearance of pirated editions of the book. Despite these setbacks, Dickens loved *A Christmas Carol*. When, in 1853, he hit on the brilliant idea of giving public readings of his work, he chose *A Christmas Carol* for the first reading on 27 December 1853, at Birmingham Town Hall. He also chose it (plus the trial scene from *The Pickwick Papers*) for his final public reading on 15 March 1870 in London.

A Christmas Carol describes the transformation of a misanthropic miser called Ebenezer Scrooge ('hard and sharp as flint, from which no steel had ever struck out generous fire') into a decent and charitable benefactor, over the course of a single Christmas Eve. He is visited by the spectre of his dead business partner, plus three Christmas ghosts, and is shown the effect that his behaviour has on others – and, in particular, on Tiny Tim, the crippled son of his ill-treated clerk, Bob Cratchit. Despite the childlike delight and relief of the redeemed Scrooge on Christmas morning, *A Christmas Carol* is a frightening and bleak story. Dickens pulled no punches about the evils that man inflicts on his fellow man: 'This boy is Ignorance ... on his brow I see that written which is Doom, unless the writing be erased.' His powerful storytelling prodded the public's conscience and encouraged them to do something about the terrible sufferings of some Victorian children.

The book also reawoke the British love of Christmas. Readers adored the idea of celebrating with merry games and plenty of food, and they also liked the notion that even the most hard-hearted penny-pincher could find redemption. Perhaps there was hope for them after all. The basic plot of *A Christmas Carol* became a recipe that Dickens rehashed, with varying degrees of success, in four more Christmas stories during the 1840s: 'The Chimes' (1844); 'The Cricket on the Hearth' (1845); 'The Battle of Life' (1846); and 'The Haunted Man and The Ghost's Bargain' (1848). He also wrote several Christmas stories that appeared in his own magazines *Household Words* and *All The Year Round*.

In Dickens's later works, Christmas casts a much longer shadow than it did in the heyday of Mr Pickwick. In *Great Expectations* (the first instalment of which was published in December 1860), it's on a cold Christmas Eve that a terrified Pip first meets Magwitch, the escaped convict. Christmas in *The Mystery of Edwin Drood*, which was Dickens's final and unfinished novel, is an equally sobering affair, with the disappearance of the eponymous Edwin on Christmas Eve.

Yet despite the darker tone of Dickens's later writings about Christmas, he will continue to be associated with the joy – and cherished memories – that this time of year can bring. As he wrote in *The Pickwick Papers*:

> Many of the hearts that throbbed so gaily then, have ceased to beat; many of the looks that shone so brightly then, have ceased to glow; the hands we grasped have grown cold; the eyes we sought have hid their lustre in the grave; and yet the old house, the room, the merry voices and smiling faces, the jest, the laugh, the most minute and trivial circumstances connected with those happy meetings, crowd upon our mind at each recurrence of the season, as if the last assemblage had been but yesterday! Happy, happy Christmas, that can win us back to the delusions of our childish days; that can recall to the old man the pleasures of his youth; that can transport the sailor and the traveller, thousands of miles away, back to his own fireside and his quiet home!

ACKNOWLEDGEMENTS

It has been a joy to write this book about my favourite time of the year, although it has been strange to be immersed in thoughts of Christmas during one of the mildest springs on record. My heartfelt thanks to Charlotte Cole, my editor at Ebury Press, to Susan Pegg and to everyone else there who has helped with the book. Many thanks, too, to Bernice Davison, for her highly detailed and knowledgeable copy-editing. I would also like to thank David Wardle for designing such a beautiful book cover for the third time running. Thanks, too, to Susan Chadwick for her botanical suggestions and research; to Wendy, Terry and Jane Harvey of The Martello Bookshop in Rye, East Sussex, for their wonderful enthusiasm and support; and also to my agent, Chelsey Fox, and my husband, Bill Martin, who both give me so much behind-the-scenes back-up and encouragement. I would also like to thank my family, both past and present, for the many cherished Christmas memories that I drew on while writing this book. God bless you, every one.

INDEX

Come, bring with a noise,
My merry, merry boys
The Christmas log to the firing;
While my good dame, she
Bids ye all be free,
And drink to your heart's desiring.

With the last year's brand,
Light the new block, and
For your good success in his spending,
On your psalteries play,
That sweet luck may
Come while the log is a-tending.

Drink now the strong beer,
Cut the white loaf here,
The while the meat is a-shredding:
For the rare mince-pie
And the plums stand by
To fill the paste that's a-kneading.

'CEREMONIES FOR CHRISTMAS',
ROBERT HERRICK